THE
TRIPLE KNOT

DESIGNING AND LEADING SUSTAINABLE HIGH PERFORMANCE ORGANISATIONS

TERRY MCCAUL

The Triple Knot:
Copyright © 2025 by Terry McCaul

Interior design: Lorna Reid - Reedsy

Names: McCaul, Terry, author

Titles: The Triple Knot
Designing and Leading Sustainable High Performance Organisations.

ISBN: 978-0-473-74219-5

CONTENTS

REVIEWS

"I found myself identifying with several of the characters from different roles and organisations I've worked in - and that's the magic of this book. It brings the tools and ideas that can work in all sorts of organisations, while also helping mirror back to us the different lenses we need to bring together to make change truly stick."

Christy Law
Senior Leader, Change Delivery

"This is the most refreshing book on Leadership, Change and Culture that I have read – an outstanding read!!!
It is grounded in reality, demonstrates the essentials that we see internationally which are required to build successful organisations in the changing and uncertain world we are in.
It is about people – not jargon - and contains lessons that are guaranteed to deliver performance, commitment and highly engaged teams. Highly recommended!!!"

Terry McCloy
Managing Director -FuturePath International
International Change, Leadership & Coaching

"Terry shares an original approach to considering the compelling leadership challenges we face in organisations today. He challenges our commonly unchallenged media fuelled tropes and assumptions to reveal some timeless truths about leading organisations, and our people. A commendable read."

Crispin Garden-Webster
Leadership Coach

"Terry weaves powerful leadership concepts for today's business world through a novel that is both engaging and instructive."

Dr Kelvin Watson
Senior Executive, NZ Public Sector

"Terry McCaul draws on his heritage and uses an ancient Celtic symbol to challenge the existing approaches to organisational development and cultural change. If you find yourself frustrated with the traditional perspectives for achieving change in your organisation, I suggest you may very well find the answers in the pages of Triple Knot."

Cillín Hearns,
Director of Results Coaching and author of 'Now, Lead Others'

"A great read that is an innovative way of presenting a concept through a story. Being on the "left brained, Non-Adaptive" side of the table, it did prompt me to think about things differently and adjust my mindset in the way I look at our business and listen to other people's ideas. "

Eugene Ng
Director - H2R Consulting

"Story telling is an ancient and powerful way to convey ideas and challenge thinking. Using a plausible and relatable business story Triple Knot nicely integrates learning with an entertaining story. If you feel like you're in a bit of a rut in your organisation, the ideas woven into the story of The Triple Knot, may just be what you need to help you break the inertia of the status quo."

Frank Moes
Human Resources Executive (retired)

ACKNOWLEDGEMENT

"Simplicity is the ultimate sophistication"
Leonardo da Vinci

This book has been in the ether for some time. When it was first suggested that I write a book that could help others to develop their leadership skills all I could think of was, "Oh God. Not another 'How to' book!"

So, eventually, I produced a novel instead. I would like to thank all of the people I have worked with over the last half century who were key players inside some of these stories and who in being so, helped me in my education and growth. I hope others can learn from the stories too.

I would like to express my deepest thanks though, to my wife, Jane. You were always by my side through both good and not so good learnings. Your patience with me as I spent most of the first half a year of my retirement, working on my keyboard has been nothing short of stupendous.

To the three amigos who gave me honest, forthright, and sometimes harsh (rightly so) feedback on my first draft, Terry McCloy, Frank Moes and Anaru Matthews. Thanks guys. I changed quite a bit from your reviews.

To everyone who reviewed this book before it went to publication; Kelvin Watson, Crispin Garden-Webster, Christy Law, Cillin Hearns, Eugene Ng. My sincere thanks and apologies for putting you through this....

Thank you also to Lorna Reid, for the book design and making it all readable as an e-book.

INTRODUCTION

The world of work and organisational life has been undergoing profound changes over the last decade. Profound change, in itself, is not new. There have been several periods of fundamental change over the centuries. The Industrial revolution, for example, and the technological revolution, are good examples of profound change. Both shifted the world of work irrevocably.

Today's changes are different. They are driven by a confluence of factors never before seen in this world. Enabled by technology, societal shifts in attitudes towards work and organisational life have created a new world, within which, leaders are struggling to understand and adjust.

In an era defined by identity politics, culture and class wars, adjusted histories, widening political divides, pandemics, and rampant misinformation, it is very difficult for organisations built around traditional operating models to flourish and thrive. People are really struggling. In fact, so much so that there is a worldwide crisis of a lack of leadership.

Leaders appear to be grasping at almost anything that popular media suggests they should be thinking about or doing.

Worthy outcomes in areas such as diversity, equity and inclusion have been devalued by poorly qualified 'practitioners' who claim to resolve issues through very dubious practices, and shallow interventions. Many of which just result in a shift of bigotry to different targets. These practices are often based on the thinnest of rationales and without any real rigour or expertise applied to their design.

Time poor, and underprepared managers and leaders do not have the capabilities to really understand or research deeper and more meaningful ways to fulfil the human needs within their workplaces. So employment relationships have become more transactional and less loyalty based. The concept of the organisation as a community has been seriously eroded by pop culture and fad.

The new world of organisational life, still emerging, needs new thinking. The old ideas are fast becoming irrelevant.

Over much of the last decade, in the western world especially, organisations have had to try and navigate enormously difficult, and often quite destructive, large scale ideology shifts. These shifts have come from many different directions, including Government policies, employee expectations, societal expectations and world events such as climate change, armed conflicts and pandemics.

There are three main factors that continue to be most worrisome in the potential for irreparable damage to be caused to organisations and their communities:

One is the lack of rigour, sense, logic and evidential research sitting behind the growth of some employment related ideologies, beliefs and practices. Many are driven entirely by misinformation and a desire on the part of some people for things to be true when they may not, actually, have any basis in fact.

Another is the relentless pace and volume of the introduction of new things. There is no time to understand, build, and adjust, so leaders are always being asked to compromise the quality of the end product or outcome.

Third, the wildfire speed at which new myths and poor practices are spread, believed and acted upon. Without thought of medium or longer term consequences to the sustainability of the organisation. This, to me, is the most damaging of all. Thousands of years of science, history, and wisdom are all pushed aside by the fervour of instant believers who shout louder and mobilise online en masse. This is exacerbated by a media system that is poorly led, partisan, and uncaring of consequence. They just want clicks.

Much of the western world's workforce is deeply unhappy. New forms of bigotry and bullying have emerged in the workplace due to very poor diversity and inclusion strategies and identity politics. Worker resilience is low, and underperformance is common. The quality of management and leadership has dropped significantly as promotion is too fast and many are not emotionally intelligent enough, yet, for the roles they are finding themselves in.

Organisations are buckling under the weight of their own non-productive hierarchies and structures. Particularly in the public sector. Bricks and mortar are no longer assets but millstones, as more employees demand hybrid and flexible working arrangements. Everywhere I look, I see entitlement and victimhood.
I do not pretend to have all of the answers but this book presents a view that I believe aspiring change agents, especially senior executives, and those who want a better, more deliberate way forward, can use to cut through a lot of the noise and focus on the really important things to enable a successful, sustainable enterprise to function and adapt to shifts that will keep coming for some time. This is not a 'How to' book.

The book describes some perspectives and core concepts that I have developed over a very long career in designing and leading major change and transformation in organisations.

It builds on the work of others such as Daniel Goleman and suggests an idea for a more contemporary style of leadership relevant to managing and leading the workforce issues of today.

The core major concept is the Triple Knot model that can be used in the design or redesign of the organisational operating model and system. This model is quite simple, and effective, but it does mean that you may need to question some of your current paradigms about how organisations function and prioritise what they do.

The great explorer Thor Heyerdahl once said, " Progress is man's ability to complicate simplicity."

I firmly believe that the time has come to make a shift and turn that around. Our maxim should read…"Progress is man's ability to simplify complexity."

I have decided to use a unique and simple, way of presenting these concepts. Through a story. A novel in fact.

The story is one which has aspects many leaders will recognise, and indeed, many of the anecdotes within are real, and have occurred. I wanted to make the book interesting and entertaining to read, as well as useful and thought provoking. You will be the judge of that and I am more than happy to hear any feedback you may have for me after reading it.

I hope and pray that you will get value out of this book and that it will help, in some way, your journey through the murky world of organisational life.

I wish you all the best.

Terry McCaul

CHAPTER 1

THE RETREAT

M oris Bąk sat down heavily into the leather armchair next to the open fire. He was tired. Not physically tired so much as bone numbing mentally knackered. He'd been really pleased when he'd accepted the job as CEO of the company. A reward for all of his hard work as CFO.

The company's finances had been in a sad state when he'd arrived three years before. The books at that time were in a bit of a mess and despite the fact that there was a lot of demand, and the place was really busy, things just never seemed to get any better. There was constant pressure from all directions to improve but he could only try and ensure that the finances were sound and that good process drove good results.

Well, the finance team had managed to make some good gains and the new system especially, had helped to ensure that the company had moved into a healthy state of responsible financial practices. It was actually doing quite well and had turned a tidy profit last year.

Even so, why did things feel so damn difficult all the time? Staff turnover was higher than ever. Everybody seemed to complain about how long things took and customer complaints just seemed to grow. The team could never get on top of things.

Now he was CEO. The buck stopped here. Leadership was his

responsibility. "You're a leader now, not a manager." He thought. How come things seemed harder? Wasn't he the boss now? Couldn't he influence things more? It felt like all he ever did was listen to whinging. He felt like an agony aunt. Not a Chief Executive.

Nope. Everyone now had a piece of him and they all wanted their take. The Board had made it clear that they wanted change across the company and especially, greater performance overall.

Staff wanted greater job security and better conditions. Managers wanted direction and guidance.

What to do? Three months in the new role and he was no wiser than when he said yes and took up the role. Self doubt wasn't getting him anywhere. Time to step up….

He sighed, "Well I think I'll start by pouring myself a glass of this fine Connemara peated…"

"Don't stop there. Your glass looks lonely."

It was Jerry, the Head of HR. He'd joined the company at around the same time as Moris and this executive retreat was his idea. In fact, he'd been pushing for this almost ever since he'd arrived.

Jerry was a bit of an enigma. He didn't quite fit the mould of the standard HR manager. He liked to espouse some alternative approaches to usual HR practice but the organisation had always been a bit too conservative for some of his ideas to gain traction. He was often quite critical of the HR sector 'dogma' as he called it.

Jerry was very popular with the staff though, and never shied away from some of the more 'negative' aspects of running a company. Moris had thought that the Board would appoint Jerry to the CEO role and was a little surprised that things weren't the other way around. Truth be told he was a little uncomfortable around Jerry these days due to this.

"Ready for battle?" Jerry asked, as he settled into the other armchair in the small alcove.

"Do you think it will be a battle then?" Moris asked as he poured a glass for Jerry. "All of our leaders get along ok don't they?"

"Oh yeah. Everyone is very nice to each other. That's a normal thing. Especially in this country. People are so polite that they can actually be oversensitive to others' feelings. That doesn't mean there won't be any battles. Most especially when people feel that their beliefs are being threatened. Just don't be too surprised by the level of passive/aggressive push back we might get over the next few days."

"Hmmm.." mused Moris. "Is there a danger we could actually upset any of the team so much that they become disengaged? Spit the dummy. Even leave?"

"Actually, yes. There is always that danger. But think of it like this. Our leadership team aren't really behaving as a team. We've discussed this. Part of it is that they have all been following their own vision as to how things should be. That's kind of fine to a point but it does mean that we are occasionally finding our teams disconnected from each other and problems crop up across the business as little thought is given to how a solution in one part of the company might impact others. You and I both know how much work the corporate units have had to do to reduce the damage caused by silo thinking in other parts of the business.

"If the senior leadership team aren't together on the vision and how things should work then we're just wasting efforts. If someone thinks they don't want to be part of it wouldn't you rather know now than find out later because somebody decided to take their unit in a different direction? That might end up in a real conflict situation. " Jerry sighed after taking a sip from his glass.

"Anyway. Really. What is there to get upset about? We are only trying to build clarity about who we are and how we operate. That's our jobs isn't it?"

"Yeah. I guess so," agreed Moris

After another sip, Jerry continued. "I remember years ago when I first arrived in NZ as a kid. A bunch of kids asked my brother and me if we'd like to play footy. We both said yes and joined them.

"Pretty quickly it became obvious that we didn't have a clue. They had a rugby ball for a start and we'd grown up with a proper round ball. They gave us a quick rundown on the rules and we got into it. I loved it but my brother hated every minute. After a while he went and sulked on the sideline. This wasn't football as he wanted it to be." Jerry smiled as he remembered his older brother's face that day.

"He never joined into a rugby game again. I, on the other hand, just enjoyed the rough and tumble and got right into it. His choice, his loss. He was sour prick anyway." Jerry smiled again.

"How many versions of 'football' do you think are sitting in the heads of your SLT? And who thinks we should be playing a different version? Worse. Who might already be playing a different version?"

"Fair enough. But I'm still nervous about this guy you've got in to facilitate. Seems a bit high powered for us."

"Don't let it worry you. I've known him for years. He's fairly easy going. He'd laugh about being thought of as being too high powered.

"He's not a facilitator who leaves people floundering through a process. It's the outcomes that are important. Honestly, the amount of facilitators I have seen who are so vested in their 'process'…We shouldn't lose sight of the fact that this is about achieving objectives. When people have a view, he'll make sure it gets discussed. He's also as vested in the success of this as anyone. Trust me. If we need to adjust the agenda, we will."

Moris sighed, "Okay. Let's see how it all plays out. Perhaps we should join the others for dinner?"

Moris was still feeling a bit nervous as he and Jerry wandered into the dining room at the chalet. He looked around. The team was all here except for Averil. That wasn't unusual for her. Averil was always late. Some emergency with the comms team no doubt. They always seemed to be in firefighting mode with some emergency or another.

Jerry had joined Leo by the large and very inviting open fire. The two of them really did look the part. Of an age they both enjoyed sports and often engaged in a banter around their favourite teams. Leo was the Director of IT and ran a pretty tight ship. He'd joined the company when he'd emigrated from South Africa about seven years ago. Over that time his team had pretty much replaced all of the core systems. His team were good. Moris wondered what Leo's future ambitions might be.

The remaining two members of the team were sitting at the end of the large dinning table and appeared to be deep in a conversation with each other. Susan, the new CFO, and Gordon, Head of Engineering. Susan seemed to be settling in ok to her new role. Bit of a shaky start as she took a while to ease up on the busyness and take time to get to know her team. Moris still wasn't certain he'd made the right decision on her yet. He wondered what she and Gordon were discussing so earnestly.

As the team sat down to dinner Moris tried to force stop his thoughts nervously tumbling toward tomorrow. He needed to relax and enjoy the company of his team this evening.

~

Kick off time for the first session was 8:30am. It was now 8:15am and Moris was already onto his second cup of coffee. He'd risen early and been for a short walk around the grounds of the centre. The small conference venue was in a beautiful setting and he felt refreshed after being out along a small forest path and surrounded by birdsong.

The facilitator, Tony, had arrived early to ensure the room set up was okay and to prepare for the day. Moris didn't really know Tony that well. He had met him. But only for about a half an hour a few weeks ago so Jerry could finalise things. He seemed like a nice guy and had a pretty impressive history.

Jerry was already here and talking with Tony, but the others had yet to show. Moris was confident that they would be on time as he'd already seen them at breakfast. Although Averil still hadn't shown up. He'd had a message late last night from the office that she would be on time for the start but had to sort out something urgent. She was sorry that she wasn't able to join them for dinner the previous evening.

Jerry re-introduced Tony to Moris. "Morning Moris. You remember Tony? Sorry we haven't really had a chance to spend more time on where all of this will take us but you have been a bit hard to nail down with your diary recently."

"Don't worry Jerry. You know I trust you and you're the expert in this so just looking forward to the next few days. I hope all is going well Tony?"

"Hello Moris. Everything is going very well thanks. I'm looking forward to working with you and the team. From what Jerry's been telling me you folks have been eager to do something like this for a while."

"Yes that's right. Jerry and I especially. We've both tried hard in the past to convince the previous CEO and the Board that this sort of exercise is not only valuable but a necessary part of running a great organisation. Not entirely sure why the company wasn't up for it until now but I'm pleased we can move forward with it."

"Great. Let's hope that the next few days live up to expectation and deliver what you need."

Tony quipped as he bent over the keyboard of his laptop and adjusted some settings for the screen.

By now the others had joined and were busy seating themselves around the table. "Still no Averil though...." thought Moris.

Soon, everyone was sitting at the table and Tony had signalled that he was all ready to go.

"Kia ora everyone," Moris started. "Just before we launch into things, has anyone heard from Averil? I'm starting to get a bit worried."

There was an awkward silence and then Leo spoke up. "I'm afraid Averil isn't coming," He said. "We thought she'd told you too." Moris shook his head and looked confused.

"Averil is leaving the company and has a new job over at Mill's," blurted out Gordon.

Moris looked over at Jerry whose surprised expression was accentuated with a large shrug. "Didn't see that coming!" he said.

Moris sighed deeply and shook his head. "Bloody hell!" he swore under his breath.

He looked around the room at faces all trying to avoid making eye contact with him. Not a great start to things. "Okay." He sighed again, " Let's move on and I'll deal with this later. Unless anyone else has any surprises for me today...?

"I'm going to hand over to Jerry to introduce our facilitator, Tony, and to outline what we have in front of us over the next couple of days. This retreat has been something Jerry has been pushing to do for some years now and I want to say that I am very supportive of this. I really hope you'll give this time the importance that it has for the team and this company. Over to you Jerry."

"Thanks Moris. Well. It's a shame to start this on a a bit of a sour note for us but I'm sure Averil is doing what she believes is best for her. Anyway, as you can see from the brief agenda in front of each of you we have a fairly open but ambitious road ahead of us. Tony is a recognised expert in his field and we are lucky to have him here to facilitate this workshop. I won't go into his entire history as it's really, really long." He grinned as he said this and looked over at Tony who just raised his hands and nodded.

"I've known Tony for about twenty years having met him when he presented to my MBA class on the subjects of leadership and strategy. Tony has worked as a senior executive across a lot of different organisations in both public and private sectors. He is recognised internationally as a thought leader in high performance cultures and organisational design and has been widely published in journals and magazines around the world. He has been a key advisor to some very senior figures including Government Ministers, Chief Executives and Governance Boards.

'I'ony says he is largely retired now but I know he is kept fairly busy and I'd like to thank him in advance for giving us his time to help us in this."

Tony stood up and thanked Jerry for his nice introduction. He took a deep breath and exhaled. "Welcome everyone. My thanks to you all for giving me this chance to work with you. Jerry has briefed me on some of the challenges you face as a company and I hope to be of some help in your journey. I will start by saying that I don't have all of the answers. No one person does, but I think the first step is for this group, the leadership team, to understand and acknowledge the questions and challenges that need addressing. That's really what these days away from the hustle and bustle are all about. Shortly I'm going to expand a little on how we might make progress against the agenda but first I would be interested to understand from each of you how you would view the next few days to be a success or not."

Tony was an adept facilitator and within a fairly short period of time the whiteboard was full. Two lists had appeared and pretty much everyone had contributed something. If he thought a person was being a bit reserved or wasn't saying, anything Tony asked them directly, politely, for their contribution.

The two lists were simply headed *"What would success look like?"* And *"What would failure look like?"*.

Moris thought to himself, "This might not be so daunting after all. A good start in getting people engaged…"

CHAPTER 2

THE COACH

I t was two weeks since the retreat. All of the team had said they had thought it a really successful exercise and they were all keen to now build plans to improve. Moris was discussing the outputs with the Board Chair. She seemed impressed with the quality of the conversations and forward objectives that had been produced as outputs from the sessions.

"Overall, we really need to try and understand the whole organisation as an operating system." Moris said. "We felt quite strongly that everything was connected and that you couldn't just fix one thing and that would be it. Tony left us with a consensus that we needed a fairly broad plan to take us forward. I guess the thing though, is where do you start? When you try and look at the system as a whole it's just so daunting. We tried to break it up a bit and spent some time digging deeper into some specific aspects but I have to say that things seem to have been working in silos for so long now that I felt we were only seeing things from our individual perspectives."

Moris shook his head and sighed. "I kept looking for a common areas of focus and the only thing that kept coming to mind was 'Culture'. That does worry me as in my experience culture is a very 'fat' subject that everyone talks about, but always seems bigger than world hunger to actually do anything with."

Maureen, the Chair, thought about this for a little while and then said, " You know Moris. I hear pretty much the same thing from other organisations I'm involved with. I have heard of your guy Tony though. It seems this stuff is where he's made a name for himself. In fact, I'm aware that his ideas so impressed a group of experts at a United Nations Conference on building sustainable organisations that he won the presenter of the conference award and was invited back the following year. Guess what. He won it again. Why don't you ask him to be more involved and help guide you along a bit? We'd be happy to fund it from the Board."

Moris sat back in his chair and smiled widely. "Maureen, I'm so glad you said that. I was going to ask if you'd be happy with me hiring him as a coach. For me. I think that change needs to be seen to be owned and driven by myself and the SLT and I think having Tony as my coach would help manage any impressions that we are using 'consultants' to do things. What do you think?"

"Excellent approach Moris. Why don't we also plan on having a small session with the Board so we can all endorse this? I think we could spend half an hour with him giving a view. Otherwise we'll likely have a little bit of push back from a couple of members if you know who I mean."

"Ok. I'll call Tony later today and see what we can set up."

"Oh, by the way. What on earth happened with Averil?"

Moris groaned and shifted in his chair. "I honestly wish I knew. She didn't say anything to me before she left."

~

"Jerry. Have you got a few minutes?" Moris asked as he passed by Jerry's office door.

"Sure. Now?"

"Yeah. Let's grab a coffee and go to my office."

After settling down into one of Moris' armchairs, Jerry asked "What's up? Is this about Averil?"

" No. Not about Averil. But we should get our heads together on that one soon anyway. I want to talk about the whole culture thing. I know you have been frustrated with the lack of support from other members of the SLT. As you and I both know, we have some issues in that space."

Moris took a deep breath and carried on. "I've decided to engage Tony as an executive coach to me but I wanted you to have a think about how that might impact your role and let me know how you might feel about it. I thought he might be useful for you as well in helping to remove some roadblocks. As far as I'm concerned this is your area of expertise and I don't want to set something up that you won't be happy with."

Jerry thought about it for a few minutes and Moris was worried that he'd perhaps this might be a bridge too far. However. He needn't have worried. Jerry's response was just what was needed.

"Are you kidding? Tony's approach might be just the thing we need to break the cycle. Look, I'm a realist about what makes change happen and in my world it rarely comes just because HR think it should. I mean, it seems as though the HR sector think we know what needs to be done but to be honest I've been pretty underwhelmed by what the business media say and what my contemporaries seem to think. Over the years this company has pretty much done everything the books suggest but hand on heart I couldn't say we've had screaming success.

"We need some real breakthroughs. I know I'm basically pushing shit uphill with a pointed stick. It's the old prophet inside story. Tony is a bit of a maverick when it comes to the subject of culture change but man he does make sense. I guess it's because his background is much wider than HR and he isn't limited by what the sector says. Most HR teams aren't game enough to question the 'rules' like he does." Jerry signalled quotation marks as he said this.

"Actually. I think it would be a great idea to have Tony as a sounding board for you so that the exec team feel less 'threatened' that one of the team has more influence than the rest. There is always that danger that HR is seen as the black robed shamans conjuring up arcane ways of controlling the CEO," he raised his eyebrows trying to look malevolent. "This could help manage that. Having said all of this I am a bit concerned at how this could affect the view of what the role of the HR team in this space might be. How do we handle that?"

"Well, I did mention culture, but actually, I really want Tony to be more of a whole of business coach. Culture is everyone's responsibility I know but I still need you and the team to be the focal point. Tony mentioned something during a coffee break that I've been thinking about. The idea that the company is a whole system and we need to understand how everything works together to be most effective. This isn't just about culture. It's about the whole thing. Our operating model. Our design. Culture is a massive part of the overall picture and I'd like to have your team focus more on that aspect as a lead. What do you think?"

"Okay. How do you see it actually working?"

"Honestly. I don't know. I thought we could start with you and I meeting with Tony and asking him."

~

So it was that two weeks later the three men found themselves in a cafe.

"So Tony. Following up with some of the things that came out of our session with the SLT. Which, by the way, I thought went really well. You and I briefly touched on some of your ideas about designing and running organisations in the modern world. In fact, my chair informs me that you have quite a reputation in this space."

Tony grinned and said "I hope it's a good one."

Moris glanced over to Jerry and continued. "I want to sound you out for some more work. More related to those ideas you have around organisation design. Can you help us?" Moris again looked over at Jerry as he said this and Jerry nodded.

"Hmmm. Look. I know I can help but you are right. I do have a reputation. But I'm aware that for some people I am too far outside the norm. Others do seem to respond positively to what I say but I have to be honest with you, when it comes to actually taking action, their risk aversion mechanisms often kick in at some point and they end up falling back to what they think is the safe path. I'm too long in the tooth to burn energy if this is only window dressing."

"Wow. You really do say what you mean don't you?" said Moris

Tony smiled. "I've been told that." He leaned forward in his chair, sipped his coffee, and looked straight into Moris eyes.

"My view is quite simple, you can't build half a boat and outsail everyone else. It's quite weird really, New Zealand has a very good record in being innovative and experimental when it comes to sports for instance, but our giant inferiority complex kicks in when it comes to running a business. There is a tendency to downplay our own thought leaders and follow advice from celebrated business schools, big International consultancies and larger overseas organisations who pour megabucks into efficiency and effectiveness programmes. We just don't back ourselves in business and it's like our confidence comes from the fact that something worked somewhere else. Tall poppies are very tall, in this country."

"Can you give me an example of what you mean?" asked Moris.

"Sure. I took up a role once as Chief People Officer of a government department. The guy who brought me in had worked with me in the past and knew how I thought and operated. He'd convinced the Executive team that it was time to be bold and step off the same old roundabout. One of the Executive team told me that they had never hired a person like me before."

Tony smiled wryly. "To be honest, I told him that I had always stayed out of the public sector because they were so risk averse and timid. He and I agreed to seriously give each other a chance.

"This organisation had a poor reputation as an employer. The Union bullied it every chance it could. Management were nice people but they were emotionally unequipped to deal with poor performers. Many staff were telling us that they were sick of how the organisation didn't address this. Especially since many of the poor performers were Union delegates.

"There was a very comprehensive Performance Management programme in this place. It was highly computer driven and had all of the components of the classic Performance cycle. You know, setting objectives, performance appraisals, improvement plans, etc."

"Didn't it work?" asked Moris. "I would have thought that would've helped manage those issues."

"Well…" frowned Tony. "Despite all of the claimed benefits. Performance Management with appraisals and all that guff, doesn't work. This is where I differ from many HR people. Who by the way, are the main advocates for that stuff. I come from a background in Quality Management where one of the principles is to drive out fear. Performance Appraisals have the opposite effect."

Moris looked over at Jerry who shrugged and nodded.

"So what happened?" Moris asked

"The HR team loved this system. They spent a lot of their time encouraging managers and staff to have objective setting sessions, feedback and reviews etc. Problem was, managers and staff hated it. Not just the technology. The whole process. I spent the first few weeks talking to as many people in the organisation as I could and asked them all if there was one thing that would make life at the organisation any better and it became pretty clear that this system was one of the biggest sources of dissatisfaction. Not just the computer system. It was the time and energy and work needed to complete the cycle each year. It was universally distrusted (except by the HR team) and as I said earlier, poor performance was never addressed."

"So what did you do?"

"I talked to the senior team. I have to say I was impressed that they didn't flinch when I suggested that we should stop doing this. That we should instead develop our managers as coaches (along a high performance sports model) and create a better, more dynamic, conversation based style of performance management. You know, we did it. I thought that was very brave of them. Nobody likes to be first to try something in the Public Sector, but others quickly followed."

"What happened?" queried Jerry

"I lost nearly half the HR team within a month. The positive feedback from both employees and managers was outstanding. We ran custom designed workshops on giving and receiving feedback. Trained managers to be coaches. We saved a bucket load of money in getting rid of licences for the software. Performance, despite the predictions of some managers and a very conservative HR, didn't drop. It improved.

"More than that, managers got much better at having quality conversations with poor performers and braver in dealing with unacceptable behaviour. We exited a fair few hard core union delegates and perennial under-performers in a few months. I even brought in one of the most successful, legendary, sports coaches in the country to present to all managers and give his views on coaching for high performance. There were grumbles from some of the longer serving managers about this but afterwards the feedback I got was that it was one of the most inspiring things they'd ever had at the agency."

" Wow. Great story."

"Sadly, it doesn't end there. After close to four years of building a strong, successful coaching culture I moved on. A new HR team got in and immediately turned the 2 day High Performance coaching course into an in-house 3 hour session. The excuse was that the university qualified OD expert who had been recently hired was more up to date with management coaching and it was cheaper to do it in house. Sorry Jerry, but it is a perfect illustration of why I have a certain view of HR generally."

"No offence taken Tony. I know exactly what you mean. A lot of these 'experts' have only got book learning from university and models based on research that is now nearly 5 years old when it is published as a textbook. What bugs me is how insistent they are that they know better than people who have been doing it for years. Personally, I'd rather be the guy that business magazines call to interview because I've been part of a radical new idea that has shifted performance significantly."

"Yes. I feel the same. I guess what I really want to get today is some sense as to how risk averse are you? If you want to have a traditional, safe but (in my view) largely ineffective strategy then I'm not going to be much help. I go back to my view that real progress is made by people who are willing to back their experience and intuition above academic study and research. In business, to stay ahead you can't afford to wait until the next Harvard Research study comes out and tells you what awesome organisations have been doing for the last five years. You need to be one of those organisations who rewrites the rules. This is what I mean about Kiwi's inferiority complex. We are held back in business by the belief that it has to be proven by someone else to work before we step forward. Strangely, our business brains don't seem to see the clear parallels between successful high performance in things like excellence in sport, and excellence at work.

"I don't mean this to sound a bit naff but I found this especially true in the Public Sector. So many highly educated people whose prejudice creates a real paradigm against widening their learning beyond the corridors of academia."

Tony shook his head and sighed as he said this.

There was silence for a moment and then Moris spoke. " Ok. I'm up for it. Now what?"

CHAPTER 3

THE SUSTAINABILITY TRIPLE KNOT

The atmosphere in the room was nervous, expectant. What did Moris have in mind for today? Results in the latest monthly report weren't great. He'd called a special Senior Leadership Team meeting just 2 days ago and told everyone that he expected them to prioritise this time.

Everyone duly did so and the whole team were waiting in the Boardroom. That facilitator guy was there as well. Gordon thought "What was his name again?"

Moris walked into the room and signalled everyone to sit down. "Thanks everyone for making this time. I know you are all busy," he said. "There is something important I need to cover and it involves all of you. I hope you all remember Tony?" there were nods around the room and a mumbled "that's it" from Gordon.

"Well, Tony has agreed to do some more work for us. Specifically, he is going to work most closely with myself and all of you, the SLT, to develop up and implement a plan for significant organisational change. Jerry's team will be deeply involved as well."

There were murmurs around the room at this and Leo spoke up, "Does this mean we are restructuring? I knew things weren't brilliant but that's a bit drastic isn't it?"

Everyone started talking at the same time. Moris held his hand up for silence. "No. It doesn't mean that, but I have to say I am not ruling out anything at this stage. It means that we are going to try and focus on shifting the organisation to become more contemporary, forward thinking and sustainable."

"What? Like reducing waste and being carbon neutral?" asked Susan. "That'll mean a lot of work for us in finance, reporting wise," she said.

"Well, we may actually do that some day but no. That's not what I intend when I say sustainable. I've asked Tony to outline some ideas for us so that we can then have a conversation from the same base of understanding. He has a much better way to describe organisational sustainability." Moris looked over to Tony and gestured for him to begin.

"Thanks Moris. Morning everyone. Good to see you all again. You might remember, Jerry's introduction of me at the retreat. I have spent a lot of my career working with organisations to build long term high performance. Over the years I have developed a number of concepts and tools to help guide thinking and hopefully mitigate complex problems that are within our scope of control.

"Over the next few weeks I would like to introduce some of these concepts and with you, develop a company-wide plan that will set us up for continued success. First though, as Moris said, I'd like to pick up on the discussion around sustainability. Ultimately, that's the aim. We want to be a high performing business. We want to be able to sustain that. What does that look like?"

You could hear a pin drop

"To help illustrate things I'd like to introduce you to a concept which is actually at the core of everything. I've developed this in the hope that it can be used to try and simplify as much as is possible, the complexities inherent in running any enterprise. Remember, there are many, many moving parts to a business and it is sometimes difficult to step back and view it as a whole system. I hope for us to get a better grasp of this as we spend collective time on it."

Tony moved over to the whiteboard as people looked at each

other. Moris watched them all carefully to see how they were reacting to the conversation. So far, a couple of frowns, but generally, everyone was attentive and appeared to be engaged.

As he spoke, Tony drew a diagram on the board. " This is what is known as a Triple Knot," he said.

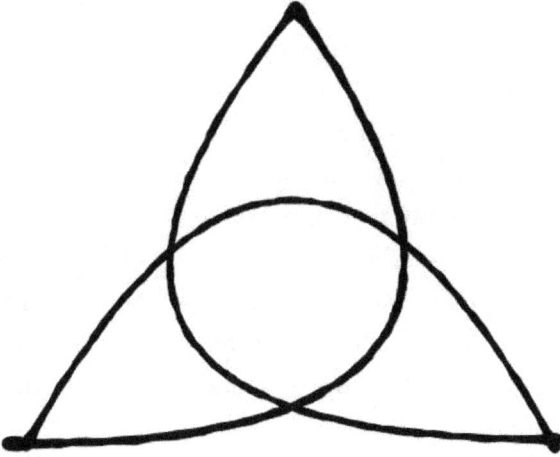

"The Triple Knot is a fairly well recognised and ancient symbol. It is most often associated with Celtic cultures. Which is probably one of the reasons I like it. Being Irish," grinned Tony.

"It signifies the relationship between any three things. It is an integral, continuous connection. For example, Birth, Life, Death. Or the three stages of life. Youth, adulthood and old age. I've heard it called the Trinity Knot or the Triquetra, but whatever it is called the concept is the same. Each area, or 'loop' denotes a factor that needs to impact the others positively for them all to flourish. If one thing isn't working well, it will bring the others down too. The place where they all intersect is where the biggest impacts occur."

Tony paused for a moment to allow everyone to think about what he'd just said before carrying on.

"Viewing an organisation through the Triple Knot gives us as a reasonably simple way of visualising any three major factors for an organisation that can be identified as critically interdependent. From an operating model view, that is really important, as often parts of the overall operating model have been designed without conscious thought as to how they will fit in the whole organisational system. There can be many Triple Knots but over the next few weeks I'm going to introduce you to four, separate, but related Triple Knots that I think are the most critical for you to get your heads around as the SLT. I think pretty much everything else falls out of understanding these Triple Knots."

Again, he paused. No one said anything but everyone appeared to be listening closely to everything he was saying.

"These aren't in any particular order of importance but the first one I want to show you is around this notion of Sustainability. Susan talked about managing waste and environmental responsibility. In a business context I believe there are three critical and interdependent areas of sustainability, for any organisation to constantly monitor, understand and address."

He went back the whiteboard and added to the diagram:

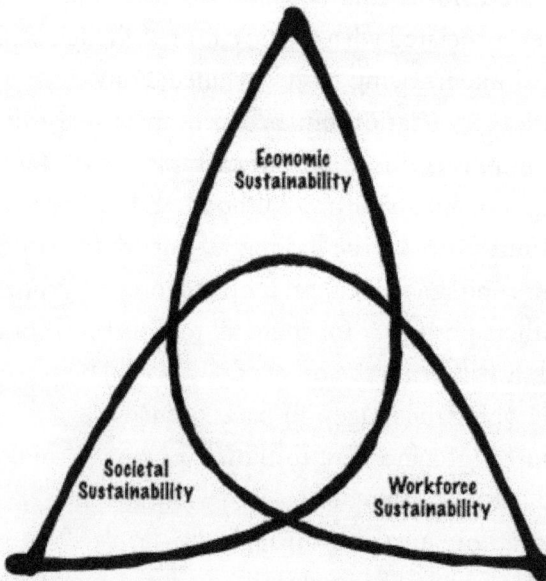

"Essentially, organisational sustainability is about leaders ensuring the company is kept healthy in these three critical areas."

Gordon raised his hand.

"Yes Gordon?" asked Tony.

"What do you mean by Societal Sustainability?"

"Well, any business venture has a range of stakeholders. From investors and employees through to customers and, well, any parties interested in what you do and how you do it. I call that your Organisational Society. It includes any of the public around places where you operate. Regulatory bodies. Groups with environmental interests. If you ignore or somehow cause damage to the needs or interests of any stakeholders within your Organisational Society. I think you put the business at risk. It's really important to consciously manage the impacts of doing business with that wider societal view as people are much more attuned nowadays to this. Acting ethically and responsibly for example, will ensure we continue to have a social licence to operate."

"Leo?" Leo had also raised a hand.

"What about operating sustainability? You know, having modern tools and technology and such?"

"That's a really good point. Remember that this is a high level use of the Triple Knot concept at this point. It's for SLT at organisation level. You can apply the concept at any level you want though. You do need the right tools, resources and people to do the work. At this stage can we view the technology, tools, process design etc as a level of detail that will come out at a later time as we discuss more of the Triple Knots and become more adept at using the concept?

"Looking at this at SLT level though, you are not going to be economically healthy if you are spending lots of money to shore up poor technology, nor are you going to have a sustainable workforce if they are frustrated that the tools they have to use aren't up to scratch. Or the capability to use them. Nothing more likely to cause frustration than tech issues.

"I think Leo, that I'd like you to keep that point in your mind as we dig deeper and look more closely at the mix of capabilities we will need to stay on top of to keep being sustainable. Are you ok with that?"

"Sure" said Leo "as long as we don't forget that we need to invest some of that money we make and stick in the bank." He looked over at Susan and winked.

"So. Are there any more questions at this point?" asked Tony.

"I have a question," said Jerry.

"Yes?"

"Can we have a break please? I really need to go to the loo…" Everyone laughed.

" Yeah. Good idea," said Moris. "Let's be back in 10." He was quite pleased with how things were going so far.

~

"Welcome back everyone," said Moris. "We have another hour here and then we can all take some time to digest things. In speaking with Tony I think it's really important for us to try and pace ourselves so that we don't get all tied up in trying to come to grips with new concepts straight away. It's an easy trap to fall into. Now. Just before we move on, I wanted to add that the Board are very supportive of us taking the time and energy to work as a team in redesigning this company to perform highly and show how that is sustainable.

"I think the three areas we talked about this morning are a great start. For me, some questions come out of the session so far," he counted them off on his fingers. "How do we know? Economic I think is relatively easy. But how do we define and measure workforce sustainability and societal sustainability? Anyone?"

"Actually," piped in Susan "I've been looking at some of the new accounting standards around environmental reporting. Things like travel and printing etc. There's also a thing called Triple Bottom Line reporting."

"Yes. I've heard of that," chimed in Jerry. "I've also been giving thought to how we can measure workforce sustainability. It's not about Health and Safety, although that is a part of it. But things like turnover, and the reasons why people leave. Investment on training, our sick leave use etc. There's lots of things."

"Okay. I guess in the absence of an Averil we should also think about how we measure our impact on customers, and society at large." suggested Moris.

"Without getting into the detail now. Could I ask you, Jerry and Susan, to get your heads together and develop a proposal on what we can do re measuring and understanding the company's sustainability performance in these three domains?"

"Sure. Yeah," said Jerry. Susan was nodding also.

"Great," said Moris. "Tony. What's next?"

"Well to be honest. I don't think we've quite got the Triple Knot concept clear in this instance. There is a danger that we can look at each of these three areas and come up with all sorts of measures, targets, and ultimately, improvement actions. Could end up with a bit of a scattergun approach. You can't do everything so you still need to prioritise.

"The point of the Triple Knot design is that you need to really define how these things are *related* to each other. This will greatly focus your thinking. Especially look at where things intersect. For example. There will be environmental sustainability items closely related to employee sustainability drivers. I'll give you an example:

"I worked in a couple of science and research organisations over a period of around 6 years. The first, was focused on climate change and protection of flora and fauna. The second focused mainly on public health risks related to environmental issues. Just after I joined, a new workers retirement savings programme was introduced. At the time many staff just saw it as a savings scheme but the leadership team saw an opportunity.

"This country isn't famous for having very strategic employment reward systems. In truth, it's not that financially rewarding to be working in science either. The pay just isn't that good. Also, these type of organisations generally don't have a heck of a lot money to throw around.

I realised that there was an opportunity to tap into something else really important to the staff that might make a bit of a difference through the reward system.

"We sourced an ethical investment fund to be our default retirement savings provider. Staff put in a percentage of salary, we matched it. We could only go up to around 4% but it was enough. Staff quickly saw that they could enjoy saving for retirement through a fund that also did good things for the planet. Trust me. That is a big incentive for an environmental scientist.

"Not only that, we used it as a selling point in sourcing research funding. This one thing had a positive effect in all three areas of the Triple Knot. It was a win, win, win situation.

"When I changed roles into the second science organisation I found that they hadn't done this kind of thinking. Staff turnover was higher, and relations between the employees and the management was much worse. Guess what we did…"

There was murmur of appreciation from around the room.

"Having the Triple Knot thinking enables us to try and find, or design, solutions that have positive outcomes in all three domains. That is the most important aspect of this concept."

'Hmm," said Jerry, frowning. "I think that puts quite a different perspective on the work you and I are about to get into Susan."

" I think so too Jerry, but I think it makes it more interesting as well," responded Susan.

CHAPTER 4

THE HIGH PERFORMANCE CULTURE

"Well," started Tony " As I mentioned earlier, organisational systems are complex. I hope that as we go through these Triple Knots you will begin to get a much better sense of the whole."

The team were now all deeply engaged in this meeting. Moris was very encouraged by what he was witnessing here.

Tony continued, "I do see a desire to dive into the detailed world of action plans and metrics but I strongly suggest this group takes the time needed to step back and collectively understand the wider implications of what we are embarking on. This will mean change. Both business wise and in my experience, very likely personally. We shouldn't rush things There'll be time for detailed planning later.

"With that in mind, I would like to spend some time with each of you individually and understand your views on how you see your role as a leader. Not today but as we go forward. If everyone is good with that I'll set up times? OK?" There was assent around the room.

"For now though I'd like to spend some time discussing another critical Triple Knot. We've been discussing how we can define sustainability and how we might sustain performance.

What we haven't really discussed though is what we actually mean by performance? Specifically, High Performance."

"Wouldn't that be tied up with our measures around

sustainability? I mean if we are making money and our staff are happy and not sick etc, and we are doing ok environmentally and all that. Seems to me if we could set some targets around these things then we focus on reaching them and that's high performance," suggested Gordon

"Seems ok to me," said Susan. "Me too," added Leo

'What about you Jerry, and Moris?" asked Tony

Moris looked at Jerry and noticed that he looked like he wanted to say something. He gestured for him to go ahead.

"Actually, I'm a bit nervous of just those measures being used as indicators of performance. I mean, if the measures are good then we are obviously doing something right. Yeah? But I have to say, and this may sound a bit strange, but results based measures don't really tell you how you are performing." He leaned forward in his chair and pressed his palms onto the tabletop. "What am I saying here…. hmmm. I play football in a Masters league every Sunday. We beat nearly everyone easily. But frankly, that's more to do with the fact that they are shit and we aren't quite as shit as them. We don't play well. In fact, we're terrible. Do you understand what I'm saying?'

"Not really. No," said Leo "But no one understands HR…" he grinned.

"Let me try," said Moris.

"Some years ago I worked for a printer and copier company. We had big targets to reach on sales of our new double sided printers. They were quite expensive printers so were difficult to move.

"We never could reach our targets until one day there was a directive that all government agencies were expected to do a lot more around their carbon footprint as the country had agreed to international targets. Now every government purchasing officer was on our back! We couldn't meet supply and sales went through the roof. Sales folk were so happy as they all got their bonuses for no extra effort." He looked around the room and saw that a couple of people still looked a bit confused.

"My point there is that we didn't do anything to perform better.

It was conditions outside of our control that gave us much better results. Couldn't really say we were high performance."

"Yeah that's better," said Leo "None of the wiffely waffle HR guff."

"Heyyy. I resemble that!" exclaimed Jerry.

'Which brings us back to the point," interjected Tony.

"What does a, HPO, a High Performance Organisation look like?"

Everyone looked around the room at each other and there was palpable discomfort as they all tried to come up with an intelligent response.

"For much of the last thirty-five years I have grappled with this question. In fact, nearly all of my roles have been focused on shifting performance rather than just maintaining a function. I have researched and studied the performance question for so long and so deeply that it's become an automatic reflex in how I view any organisation.

""Why am I telling you this? Well, it's to set the scene for what else is to come I guess. The time and energy I've devoted to this has taught me many things. One of those things is that, what a High Performance Organisation looks like today, is unlikely to be what it looks like tomorrow. The goals keep moving as the world changes its expectations."

There were a lot of nods at this statement. Tony decided to press on.

"High Performance Organisations, HPOs, mostly do hit the goals and targets they set. They are also beasts that you are confident will continue to do it, again and again. The key question is, how do they keep doing this?

"As I said, I've done a lot of work in this area. So have others. You won't be surprised to learn though that there is a general consensus nowadays that it ultimately comes down to a couple of things," he paused for effect. "Organisational culture. Quality of leadership."

Tony stopped speaking and looked about the room. Everyone was looking at him and nobody was giving anything away about how they felt about this proclamation.

Eventually, Moris spoke up "Any thoughts? Anyone?"

"Hmmph," went Leo. "I guess I'm a just a little deflated. I thought there was some big secret that we were going to learn and..well you know…get out there and do it!"

Moris looked over to Tony who took a deep breath and looked down at his shoes before glancing over at Leo and then at Jerry.

"Okay. Let's make this more real. More….tangible. Less wiffely waffley HR guff. Yes?"

Leo laughed. Jerry pursed his lips and looked up to the ceiling.

"It's really not that helpful to most people when they hear the "It's all about culture" speech.

But can I just ask, how would you describe the culture here? Is it a High Performance Culture? Indulge me."

"I think we have a really good culture here. Everyone is polite and nice and friendly to each other. Never really any big hoo hah about anything," suggested Gordon

"But is that a, *High Performance Culture*?" Tony pointed upwards with one finger. "Look. I won't keep asking questions like this but remember the Triple Knot?" there were nods. "Here's another application of it.

"Claiming that culture is the key to High Performance is not a new thing. It's been around for decades. In fact during the 1980s there was so much corporate noise about building strong, winning cultures to make your company successful that it eventually drove two Harvard researchers, James Heskett and John Kotter, to undertake a fairly comprehensive study to prove whether or not there actually was a link between culture and organisational performance. It's pretty old now of course but since that piece of work, pretty much all other studies have just reinforced what they learned.

"At that time everybody was pushing the idea that all you needed was to build a strong culture. Kotter and Heskett's research actually showed that a 'strong' culture didn't necessarily mean great performance. Some people still think it's the secret. In fact, it could have the opposite effect to high performance."

Tony paused for a brief moment as he gazed out of the window to his left.

"When I started my apprenticeship. Yes it was last century… I worked within a very strong culture. No one could honestly claim that it was High Performance though. At the Construction and Maintenance branch of the Post Office we pretty much did everything as it suited us.

"Knowledge and beliefs. How to behave etc were all passed from one generation to the next and had been working much like that for nearly a century. I loved working there but I can see now how cruisey it actually was. Unless there was a major emergency or something. In which case we really got into things. It was a very strong culture but there was a lot wrong with it as well.

"The real downside to strong cultures is that they can easily develop poor behaviours such as over-bureaucratic focus and lack of ability to adapt and change. I don't want to sound mean but I have found this in many public sector organisations. Rules and bureaucracy can often be more important than adjusting to meet the needs of customers.

"Kotter and Heskett actually found three major aspects of culture that were important in High Performance." As he spoke, Tony counted the aspects off on three fingers, "The first factor was an ability to adapt, the second was an ability to stay relevant and be strategically appropriate, and the third was, no surprise, strength of conviction to the other two.

"In my experience too many 'culture change programmes' focus on only one aspect and end up being the BBQ with lots of sizzle and no sausage. A lot of them also focus on how people feel, and engagement, rather than on performance and achievement. I have to say, if anyone asked me how I felt about working at the Post Office I would've told them it was awesome. Don't change anything. I could do pretty much what I want, when I want. I could play my football on a Saturday and still get paid for a half day overtime…. At time and a half! I was super engaged."

"I take it you don't really like culture programmes?" said Jerry "You sound a bit critical."

"Don't get me wrong. There are some good things out there but, yes, I am quite critical of many of these programmes. They are like paint by numbers exercises and seem to assume that organisations are all alike. That's like saying that all communities are the same! This just results in lot of mimicking of other people's business models and ultimately experiencing disappointment and disillusionment. There's also a fair bit of snake oil out there."

Tony looked up at the clock on the wall.

"Look. I'm really conscious of your time but this is one of the most critical concepts for us to think about so if you are happy I'd like to just show you this Triple Knot so you can get some idea of the challenges in front of us. "

Moris looked around and could see that everyone looked like they wanted to continue. "Let's keep going," he said to Tony.

" Ok," said Tony. 'I'll try not to lecture anymore though," he grinned.

"I have developed this model which has proven to be very successful over the years where I have applied it. This is the High-Performance Culture Triple Knot, and it considers those three main areas of culture that are essential for success. It really comes down to careful and deliberate design with all three areas in mind interdependently."

Tony drew up a Triple Knot similar to the one he had done earlier. It had different labels though.

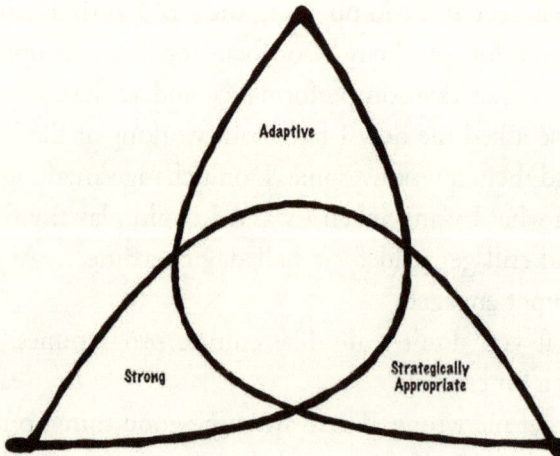

Adaptive

Strong

Strategically
Appropriate

"Does anyone remember the key features of the Triple Knot?" he asked.

"Yes," said Gordon. "There is a continuous and interdependent relationship between these three things."

"Excellent!" said Tony. "Now let me just describe what we mean by each of the three loops here. I'll start with the Adaptive Culture. "

Tony produced two flipchart pages. One headed up *Non-Adaptive* and the other headed up *Adaptive*. He stuck them up on the whiteboard. One on the far left - The Non-Adaptive, and the other on the far right side of the board.

"Kotter and Heskett found a number of core organisation behaviours, mostly evidenced by the behaviours of managers and leaders. That's important. Most Culture programmes focus on employees rather than leadership who are, after all, the climate control of the enterprise. I won't go into the actual detail that they wrote up in their excellent book but I urge any of you to read it if you get a chance. Over the years I have refined their list a bit more from my own experiences and learnings.

"Essentially, Non-Adaptive cultures are quite bureaucratic in nature. Lots of rules and policies and processes for decision making. They often seem to have a lot of hierarchy. Staff also often complain of micromanagement, " he wrote *BUREAUCRATIC* under the Non-Adaptive heading. Everyone looked at each other a little sheepishly. "In contrast, Adaptive businesses are more *RELAXED.* " He wrote that word on the opposite sheet under the Adaptive heading. " Management show a willingness to step back, not sweat the small stuff, and allow staff to do their thing without much, if any, intervention. Guidelines rather than rules and policies, are used in helping people to understand how they might do things." Pretty soon the two sheets of paper were filled and the whiteboard had two columns.

NON – ADAPTIVE	ADAPTIVE
Bureaucratic.	Relaxed
Reactive	Proactive
Risk Averse	Experimental and Learning
Closed to new ideas	Attentive to new ideas
Information poor	Informed and knowledgeable
Controlled workforce	Empowered employees
Business Results Driven	Stakeholder focused

"This is not saying that everything under Non-Adaptive is bad and everything under Adaptive is good, however. You really would want your finance team to be a bit risk averse!" quipped Tony. "You also wouldn't want your engineers to be too relaxed about meeting, or not meeting, set quality standards."

He glanced at the clock again. "I think we are about to run out of time this morning but I'm back in next week. If Moris is happy perhaps we can just finish off our discussion about the High Performance Culture model then."

Moris, looked around and saw that everyone looked about done. "Okay. Let's do that."

"Ah, before we do close though…" said Tony. "Can I just ask each of you to have a think about which side of the whiteboard describes us, here. Mostly. Are we more Non-Adaptive or Adaptive? It would be good to get a sense against each of these contrasting behaviours. We can discuss each of your thinking when we get back together."

"Thanks everyone," said Moris. "I'll send out a meeting request for …Thursday next week."

～

INTERLUDE

Later that evening Moris was reflecting on all of the conversation with the management team that morning. He felt good about it but he couldn't get a niggly thought out of his mind that there was something he was missing.

Like the team seemed to be quite engaged. He didn't get any sense that anyone disagreed with anything, but there was something nagging at him. Yet it seemed so simple. The way Tony had used the Triple Knot and the conversation about sustainability was clear.

"I'll talk to him about it tomorrow," thought Moris, and having come to that decision he sat back, relaxed into his armchair and picked up his book to read. Ironically, after all the talk of the Celtic Triple Knot, the book was about the legendary Irish warrior, Finn MacCool. Moris chuckled to himself and thought that Tony would definitely see a funny side to that.

~

It had been a tough morning. Jerry thought. After his team meeting, one of his staff had told him that she thought the idea of Triple Knot was rubbish. It hadn't been validated like the programme of culture change that she thought they should be putting in. It wasn't what Organisational Development experts she knew would recommend. All he could think about was what Tony had said about HR and paint by numbers. He'd have to think of a way to deal with this or Shona would likely impede progress. An unconscious terrorist he called her.

Jerry could really see something in the Triple Knot design. It felt right somehow.

Jerry's thoughts shifted to the gossip that he'd heard that Averil was badmouthing the business on social media. He knew he would have to do something about that. The company's reputation as an employer had been sorely damaged by the previous CEO and they were only just starting to see improvements. It was tenuous enough and Averil should know better. It was really disappointing when a former colleague was shooting at you from the sidelines.

He sighed, and decided that in the morning he would call up the company lawyers so they could start with a cease and desist letter perhaps. Ah, the joys of HR....

~

Gordon reached into his fridge for another beer. He was feeling a bit unfit and a little guilty that another beer wouldn't really help but ever since Izzy had passed he just didn't have the will to get into an exercise regime of any sort. The two of them used to be so active. They'd race each other on their bikes and man! Izzy could run for bloody miles. He'd struggle on and she'd match his pace but he knew that was all just to make sure she didn't hurt his pride.

Eight months three days and nine hours. God. He knew he had to stop this. Move on. But everything was a drag. He just couldn't find the energy to get into anything. Now they had this consultant bloke...seemed ok but that was Jerry's kind of stuff. Engineers thought in a more practical, logical way. Still, Susan seemed to think there was something in this.

Thinking about Susan just made him feel a bit more guilty so he took a big swig and sat down to watch the rugby on the TV.

~

"Jesus, Mary and Joseph!" exclaimed Leo as the squash ball hit high on his left buttock. "What the f…"

"Ahh, quit yer whingepipe," retorted Darren, Leo's opponent. "Yer squealing like a wee bairn who needs her nappy changed!" he quipped in his broad Glaswegian drawl. 'Wha's the matter wi' ye? Yer no concentratin on the game. Ye cannae just stand in front of the shot."

Leo was furiously rubbing his backside. Darren had a mean backhand.

"Anyway. Tha's stroke. And match," said Darren, reaching for the door.

As they walked out toward the changing rooms, Leo still wincing, Darren asked, "What's going on. That was an easy win. Ye played like a sassenach bagpiper t'nite."

"I dunno," said Leo. "We've got this consultant guy working with us to help improve the overall performance of the company. I'm struggling a bit with what he's talking about. You know it seems to be some of that HR lingo. I'm not good with that. He's asked us to think about a couple of things and I really don't have a clue where to start."

"Nae guid tryin to get help frae me on that. You know I'm a sales guy doncha? We got nae time for that rubbish. Why don't ye ask that coroner guy ye got at the office. Seems the two o' ye get on well. Even though ye both havnae a clue aboot football."

"Coroner guy?"

"Aye. HR. Human Remains." They both laughed as they entered the changing rooms.

≈

Susan sat staring at the computer screen. Some of these numbers just didn't add up. She couldn't get things to reconcile and she was a bit worried that either she was missing something and had made errors, or, there was something more sinister going on at the office.

She'd dug back several months and things seemed to have gone a bit skew-whiff about four months ago. Not long before she started at the company. Was Moris doing something he shouldn't? He was the previous CFO. Was there just an error at an earlier period that had compounded?

There was definitely a problem though. She couldn't account for around $75k. She'd have to go deeper into all of the budgets over the last quarter. Should she tell Moris? Or perhaps Jerry?

Maybe Gordon? No. She liked Gordon but really didn't know him all that well. It could just as easily be him who was the issue. Oh dear, what to do?

"Auntie Sue. Are you in the kitchen?" her six year old nephew Sean was in the lounge. "Yes I'm here Sean. Your dad will be around to pick you up soon. What do you want?"

"Just checking," he said. "You're too quiet."

Her sister Jackie was away working on movie set in Peru for a while and so Susan was looking after Sean every other week.

She decided to put the screen away for a while. It was Jackie's ex husband David's turn to have Sean for the rest of the week and she wanted to spend as much fun time with Sean as she could. She would get onto this work issue later.

CHAPTER 5

The following day Moris had an appointment with Tony to start the individual coaching sessions. He wasn't really sure how it was going to go and felt a bit nervous about it. They were going to meet in a cafe so as not to be disturbed and then later Tony would be around the office talking to each of the SLT.

He was on his way out the door when Jerry poked his head in.

"Got a minute?" he asked.

"Well not really. I'm heading out to see Tony but just quickly, what's on your mind?"

"Not critical. Let's catch up later. Don't want to keep the grumpy old man waiting. Please tell him I said that…" he grinned.

~

"Hi Tony," said Moris as he sat at the table in the cafe. "What can I get you?"

"No. It's on me," said Tony

"Ah ok. I'll just have a flat white thanks."

"Done."

Tony waved the waitress over and ordered the flat white and a large Americano.

"So today is the official start to your coaching sessions," said Tony.

"Yes," said Moris. "But to tell you the truth I'm really not sure how this works…"

Tony smiled. "Hey, don't worry. Neither am I." Moris looked confused.

"Look," said Tony. "There are many views on coaching and many people who do it. Some are really good and some …well, they have got an online certificate from some unheard of place and suddenly they are out there helping people achieve their 'Best Self' with their six step process for success in leadership, or something like that."

He played with the placemat on the coffee table and looked over the rim of his spectacles at Moris. "I don't really know what you expect, but my preferred way of coaching isn't to follow a set process or model like many do. I can't help a person unless I take the time to understand them and what makes them tick. Each person is different and so my start point really is to find out what would tell you this is worthwhile. What do you want to get out of this and how much input would you like from me? You need to be in the drivers seat. Not me. One thing I will say though is that I am not one of those 'life-coaches' things. I think they can be dangerous to people. Honestly, every day I see another real estate agent and part time life coach advertising in the local rag.

"I'm about coaching for performance, not emotional or spiritual counselling. If that is needed in your case, I'd recommend where you could get qualified professional help.

"On the performance coaching front I tend to think of coaching more like in sports terms rather than management coaching. It's been a very long time since I curled a ball into the net from a free kick. The kids nowadays are better at it than I was and the technology of the ball and boots is far superior to what I used. I wouldn't try and coach them on how to make the ball turn. I would though, spend time with them trying to figure out and overcome what might be preventing them from doing it as well as they are able to. I'll do this by asking lots of questions and by encouraging the player to try and think how they might change things. It's better to enable them rather than make them dependent on me."

Moris wasn't quite sure what to say so he just let Tony continue.

"It's much the same with executives. You know how to do many different things. Sometimes though, you just can't seem to get the mix right. Context has a lot to do with this. As a coach, I might be able to help you view things in a certain way, adjust an approach, I could even offer some technical knowledge of areas you feel less confident about, example, employment relations, although you have Jerry for that. Pretty much it's over to you to think about what's bugging you to put on the table and see if I can help. How's that for you?"

Moris thought about this for a moment and then said, "Ok. Where do I start?"

"Wherever you like," grinned Tony

"Before we do…." started Moris, "The sessions you are having with the team. I think they're going quite well but of course they aren't saying much. What you're giving us though is much greater than the facilitation we started off with. I think I can see most of where you are going with it but I am a bit nervous that the team are still not quite sure. I think we should keep going down the Triple Knot path but we will need the board to be engaged and the SLT to click a bit more with it. Can we set up that board session as soon as possible? Is there anything you can send to them for pre reading? What's your thoughts on that?"

"Yeah. To be honest I have felt as though I've been perhaps overstepping the brief a bit but your company is absolutely in the right space for this to have major impact and I can't help myself. It's a drive I've always had to help leadership teams operate at a deeper level than what I've been observing over the last decade. I actually call it Deep Leadership.

"Leadership has become commoditised and transactional over the last few years and for it to become truly effective people in leadership roles need to start spending a lot more of their time 'on' the organisation rather than 'in' it. If you know what I mean. I think Triple Knot thinking helps them to do this."

Tony paused for a moment, one finger tapping his lower lip. "I haven't really got anything written to send to the board members but I could pull together a set of slides which I could send in advance, and then run through with them. How much time will they give me to show them?"

"No more than half an hour I'm afraid," said Moris

"Phew," sighed Tony and smiled, "I thought you were going to say "not much!" Now. How do you want to go ahead today?"

"Tell me more about Deep Leadership. I don't want to stay in the shallows. You've just pointed out my biggest concern. I spend way too much time 'in' rather than 'on' the business"

❧

Board day.

Moris had managed to get Maureen, the Board Chair, to schedule Tony in for 45 minutes as another item had not been ready for discussion and so had fallen off the agenda.

Maureen set the scene and introduced Tony to the four other board members.

"I'd like to introduce Tony Delahunt." She nodded toward Tony who was seated beside Moris. "I know a little of Tony's work, although he and I haven't met before. Tony presented some ideas to a UN intergovernmental conference in Oslo some years ago and my sister was an attendee. She actually raved about his presentation."

Tony looked a little surprised at this.

"As you'll all recall, we discussed bringing in some expertise to help Moris and his team to reinvigorate the business. Make it more contemporary, and far more sustainable. And, of course, lift performance to new levels. Tony is here to share a little of his approach and hopefully allow us an opportunity to get a greater understanding, and therefore be able to give greater support, to the work. Thank you Tony, for coming along today and sharing your thoughts with us."

With that, she gestured for Tony to begin.

"Thank you Chair, for those kind words. I wasn't aware that your sister was at the Oslo conference but I am happy that I was able to have a positive impact. Please give her my regards. Also, thanks to the Board for giving me this time in your busy day.

"Now. I have put together a small set of slides and I am aware that they have been included within your board pack.

"I won't attempt to bore you by going through the slides as I am sure you have looked at them already. I will instead just use a couple of them to help understanding. Can I ask first though if anyone has any questions?" he waited …. "No? Ok then." Tony looked at the faces of the Board members and smiled.

"I have been in the workforce for just on five decades now. In that time I have accumulated a great deal of learning and knowledge that no amount of training courses or book reading can emulate. I am of course, familiar with many models of organisational development but I know that it is important to you that the ideas I put forward are based in real world experiences rather than only from a theoretical base."

He paused to catch his thoughts and then resumed.

"I think everyone would agree that the world within which organisations conduct business has become increasingly complex and more difficult to navigate effectively. Over the last decade pandemics, natural disasters, scarcity of talent, and societal shifts in childcare, work/life balance and a myriad of other things have all contributed to a massive change in employee expectations about organisational life. Technology has greatly enabled the hybrid and remote worker and organisations have been struggling to understand and secure the right mix of assets and capabilities needed to function in the new environment.

"In the past, organisations have developed along many paths but one thing is clear. Those organisations who invest real time and effort into well considered, deliberate and ongoing system-wide design, in the longer term, consistently outperform those who just 'follow the rules'.

"By system-wide, I mean all aspects and dimensions of an organisation. System thinking isn't new. I have found most organisations really struggle with it and due to a range of factors, mostly associated with short term focus, ill-equipped leadership teams, and lack of real knowledge. Organisations can't optimise all of the moving parts together in such a way as to consistently reach and sustain High Performance.

"I have developed a concept known as Triple Knot design, that enables a leadership group to focus on the important few things that together, drive the desired outcomes. Triple Knot thinking helps leaders to cut through complexity and understand the critical interdependencies throughout the business, and specifically design them to work together. Most organisations, just assume they do.

"I have actually started to float the concepts with the team here, and even though it is early days I have been encouraged by the level of interest shown by them."

At this Moris nodded and said "Yes, I have too. The team seem to be starting to think about common goals rather than about just their own business units. Tony."

"I won't take you deeply into the actual concepts right now as it does take some time to grapple with parts of it but I am happy at any time of course to do so. Today, I wanted to give you more of a sense that what we are going into is new and different. But it is based in actual practice as opposed to pure academic theory."

One of the board members, Brian, raised a hand. Tony nodded toward him.

"What's wrong with academic theory?" he asked "A lot of businesses have had very successful results from implementing such."

"I'm not suggesting that there is anything wrong with academic theory but to quote Immanuel Kant; "*Theory without practice is empty; practice without theory is blind*". You need both.

"Let me add my simple philosophy on this though. Most academic material I have read, regarding management and effective organisations is based in research. The research and subsequent findings, generally takes around five years to emerge. Generally it is done by academics looking at practices within organisations .

"Think, 'Good to Great' for example. Awesome book for any leader to read. But it showed what great organisations were already doing. Basically that put those businesses 5 years ahead of the academic thinking. If all you are doing improvement-wise is based on ideas based in academic research then you may have already missed the bus. Your competitors could already be ahead."

"So what would you like from us?" asked Maureen

"I'll answer that" chipped in Moris. "I'd really value the board's support in this. It isn't something to be taken lightly. It will mean culture change, the adoption of new thinking, and new ways of doing things. It will undoubtably mean questioning some long held beliefs and likely there will be some resistance to this. It means, in short, change. That means I will be seeking your patience, and possibly forgiveness, on the odd occasion, as we go forward."

Maureen looked around at her Board compatriots.

Sue spoke first. "I have had a lot to do with organisations going through major change. We shouldn't take this lightly. Having said that, we can't ask the team to improve performance without giving them the space and tools to achieve that. I really like the fact that you have an on the ground track record Tony. I say let's take a deep breath and jump in."

"Any other comments or questions?" asked Maureen.

No one spoke. "Okay then. All in favour of the recommendation from Moris to go ahead as per the Board proposal say aye."All voted in favour. "Guess it's over to you Moris."

"Thank you for a very interesting session Tony."

Later that same day, Maureen, Moris and Tony were having a chat over coffee in Moris' office.

"Well Tony. You've got a lot on your shoulders here. As has Moris I might add." she said looking at both of them.

"Well. I agree… to a point I think," said Tony. "You know the old Kurt Lewin thing of -unfreeze, change, and refreeze?"

"Yes I know it," said Maureen.

"I think the unfreezing bit can be the biggest challenge but it feels to me that the main people to drive this are on side and that makes things easier."

"You may be right but I'll echo something Jerry said to me right at the start and that was not to underestimate the amount of passive/aggressive push back we will get. He suggested that early on people will be polite and agreeable as that is a culture here. I fear he may be right," remarked Moris

They all stared down at their drinks.

"So what happens now?" asked Maureen

"We have a session with the SLT on Thursday to talk about the culture of the organisation. Tony has shown us a Triple Knot called the High Performance Culture and he wants us, the leadership group, to have a discussion about how we look relative to that model. I'm quite looking forward to hearing everyone's views," Moris declared.

"Yes but building on what Jerry said we will need to ensure we get really honest comments back," advised Tony

"A lot of the early work that we do is really around bringing people up to a comfortable and consistent level of knowledge, so I'm afraid I will be stepping through a few more learning sessions with the SLT before we take it much further. Again, to Jerry's point. We need to give people space and opportunity to get onboard , or not, as the case may be, before we ask them to collectively lead change," stated Tony.

Just then there was a knock at the door and Jerry poked his head in. "Sorry to disturb you folks but do you have a minute Moris? I've been trying to catch up with you all week but this can't wait now."

"Ah. OK. You two can stay here for a while if you like. I'll nip down to Jerry's office."

"No that's ok," said Maureen. "I have to go anyway."

"Me too," said Tony. "I have to go and watch my grandson in his first actual swimming competition."

"Right. OK Jerry, come on in."

Jerry came in and sat opposite Moris who looked quizzically at him, as he waited until the door had closed behind Maureen.

Jerry exhaled loudly, puffing out his cheeks. "Bad news I'm afraid."

Moris closed his eyes and took a long deep breath through his nose. "Tell me…"

CHAPTER 6

HOW DO WE RATE?

"You have to make time for yourself. I don't want you to go burning out like Edward did. You know this," asserted Fiona, Moris' wife.

Moris was stretched out on his recliner armchair with Hoover, his Westie, lying on his back over Moris' knees. Hoover loved having his tummy rubbed and Moris was always willing to help in that regard.

"How is Edward by the way? We haven't heard from him for a while."

Edward was Fiona's brother and he had experienced some mental health issues over the last two years. Everyone said it was burnout due to his stressful job but Moris suspected he'd had issues for a long time and probably should have had help many years ago.

Fiona glared over at Moris. "He's still the same. Donna says he is improving but I think it must be a wishful thinking. Now we're talking about you not Edward remember."

Moris chuckled, "I'm fine. Really. Just lots to do. Actually I'm better than fine because most of what we need to do is really positive creative work. It's energising."

"Well. Work's over for the day so why don't you put on some music and relax."

"Great idea," said Moris. "How about some Van the Man."

"Okay but let's have Veedon Fleece. I really love the haunting Celtic flavour of that."

Celtic! It was bloody everywhere! thought Moris to himself as he smiled and continued to rub Hoover's tummy. Tomorrow he could concentrate on the Averil issue that Jerry had come to see him about.

～

"Ok Jerry," Moris said. "Run me through the Averil story again so that I have it all right."

"Right. Mara, our HR co-ordinator spotted that Averil was slagging us off on social media. I'm still connected to her Facebook so I had a look and sure enough she's been pretty vocal on there claiming we bullied her into leaving her job.

"Same on LinkedIn. None of it is true I think but we do need to address it. Firstly I dropped her a text and asked her to stop doing this. I also suggested that she and I could grab a coffee and she could help me understand more about why she is saying these things. She basically told me to f@*k off."

"Nasty. Something's not right. It doesn't seem like her."

"No. It doesn't. Anyway, I called up Wiremu at People Law and asked him to send her a Cease and Desist Letter. He did that and this morning we've had a response from her lawyer claiming constructive dismissal and bullying. She hasn't told us who the alleged bully is but her letter infers that you have dismissed Averil because she complained."

"What! Seriously? This is the first I've heard of any bullying and I certainly haven't dismissed anyone. We never even had a conversation as to why she didn't turn up to the retreat. What the hell is going on?"

"I don't know but Wiremu has drafted up another letter for me to have a look at in response to her lawyer. He is telling her that we will investigate but in the meantime she needs to stop spreading any more things that are damaging to our reputation. He's confident that it will stop but then we need to look into her claims. I might need to get an external to do that. Wiremu has a partner who is qualified to carry out these sort of investigations."

Moris nodded. "Okay. We need to get onto this quickly before any more damage might get done. In the meantime, are we able to post any statements to refute or whatever?"

"We can't really refute anything until we have investigated but I'll draft up a statement to settle things down a bit. Hopefully none of our other staff or major customers have seen anything. We haven't had any questions from any of them yet. It's a damn good job that Mara saw this stuff and flagged it to me. She's a talent for the future in HR. We're lucky to have her."

"Yes. I agree. See if you can use this as an opportunity for her to learn as well. Maybe have her riding shotgun with the investigator. In the meantime, just keep me posted. And thanks for dealing with it for us."

They both got up and headed out to the main meeting room where Tony and the rest of the team were waiting for the next session.

"Hi guys," said Leo. "Everything OK? You look like somebody stole your pickup truck and dog."

"Everything's fine," said Moris. "Just the usual people issues. It'll get sorted." As he glanced around the room he noticed Susan quickly look downwards and purse her lips. "I wonder what that's about?" he thought.

Tony was ready with the same flipchart lists from the last meeting but this time he had drawn a horizontal line between the two columns. The line had a Zero marked in the middle and was divided up into a 1-5 scale going outwards from the zero on both sides.

"Sorry folks but are we ready to continue?" He asked looking about the room.

"Right. Everybody remember the Non-adaptive and adaptive characteristics? Yes. Good.

I asked you to have a think about how you might describe us. To help I've put this scale in. On the far left side it goes from 5 down to 0 and on the right it goes from Zero up to 5

| 5 | 4 | 3 | 2 | 1 | 0 | 1 | 2 | 3 | 4 | 5 |

NON – ADAPTIVE	ADAPTIVE
Bureaucratic.	Relaxed
Reactive	Proactive
Risk Averse	Experimental and Learning
Closed to new ideas	Attentive to new ideas
Information poor	Informed and knowledgeable
Controlled workforce	Empowered employees
Business Results focused	Stakeholder focused

"So the scale goes 0-Neutral; 1-A bit; 2-Somewhat; 3-Mostly; 4-Very; 5-Extremely

You should only mark one side of the scale for each pair of factors.

"It isn't hugely scientific but I will ask why you have rated an item as you have. The major reason for this is to generate a conversation and understand as a group how we all view things.

"Let's start with a relatively easy one. How would you rate us in terms of being, say, Risk Averse vs Experimental? Are we more to the left on the scale or to the right? Anyone want to give me a start?"

"Ok. I'll qualify this by saying that I think it might be different in the various business units given what we do," suggested Jerry. " I would give us a 2 on the side of Risk Averse."

"Me too," said Susan "But remember, I haven't been here that long."

"Does anybody score anything on the Adaptive side?" queried Moris.

Everyone looked around at each other but no one spoke up.

"Really? Seems like we may have some work to do." said Moris.

Jerry spoke up. "It seems to me, and correct me if I'm off track

Tony, but you're not saying that Non-Adaptive is bad and totally Adaptive is good right?. You said you really would want your finance team to be a bit risk averse!"

"Well. Yes, to a degree Jerry. It is important to recognise that there needs to be the right balance between Non-Adaptive elements and Adaptive elements within the organisation given that it operates within a regulatory environment and is part of a wider ecosystem. It is really important though to have a conversation at this leadership level to understand what this means and where you would like to be rated. You might find business units have slightly different emphases but it is important that in terms of the whole company the leadership team has a consistent idea of where you want the overall rating to sit for each of these elements."

He looked around the room and could see that some people looked to be having difficulty with this.

"Right. This is often a point where people struggle. Let's try something...

"All of you have told me in our individual meetings that the company is ridiculously information poor in that we have no clear and consistent sources or flow of critical information.

Leo, you told me your team don't always get all of the information they need to make sure that the technology is doing the job that others need it to do?"

"Yeah. I did say that."

"Okay, let's try a bit more specific. For example...when a new employee starts they expect to have the tech needed to do their job pretty much straight away but you've told me that's a bit a of a sore point for your team."

"Yeessss," Leo made a face. "Too often the right information doesn't get to us on time to set up the laptop and get the licences all signed off and stuff. Sometimes we don't even get the information and we end up with an angry manager and new staff member pushing us to do an 'urgent' job. It's really frustrating for my team and, no offence Jerry, but your team has been told about this many times and things haven't improved."

Jerry looked flustered, "Well, it would really help if managers gave HR the information in the first place! I get really tired of my team being the scapegoat for managers not doing their jobs properly. Even last week we had a situation where a new employee and the manager came to payroll to demand their money as they hadn't been paid. Payroll actually had NO record that the employee even existed! Thankfully, the team solved the issue but c'mon Leo you know this happens more than it should."

" It would help if HR gave managers simple to use processes! All the paperwork…."

"Firstly, that …paperwork is mostly requirements of government. Tax and superannuation etc. Perhaps your team could look at giving us some real HR technology that works. That might make a difference."

Things were starting to get hot.

Moris decided it was time to end this. "Okay. Okay. That's enough. No one is trying to do a bad job but blame throwing isn't going to result in improvement."

"Let's have a break," he suggested.

During the break Moris and Tony chatted.

"I didn't expect that," said Moris "Those two normally get on well. That looked a little uncivil. Why do think they had that exchange?"

"Pure frustration. And because everyone views work processes from their own perspective. Your managers are trying to get their teams do the best that they can but they have designed their team processes to deliver things from the point of view of their area without necessarily thinking about the wider organisation needs. As you heard, Leo didn't seem to appreciate that Jerry's team has a responsibility beyond the information he needs to get a laptop up and running. Probably never even thought about it.

"This is the underlying stuff that drives culture and limits performance. To be frank, if it isn't addressed at this level then it's no surprise that teams don't work well across business unit boundaries.

"Most management don't think about work in whole of system way. They think about it from a silo perspective of the area they manage. I'm sure both of them want to do a good job but what 'good' looks like to either of them has been different in each of their minds. I know it got a little feisty but now we have a very real example to look at how behaviours affect the company's ability to have an adaptive culture.

"Both Jerry and Leo have said their teams don't get the right information to do their jobs. That's one of the key elements of an Adaptive culture. Remember?"

" I see what you mean. So what do you think we do? Knock heads together and make them work better together?" asked Moris

" If only that would work….It is a good example though of why we need to be more deliberate about culture. A lot of things can be resolved early on if there is a culture of collective responsibility, especially at senior level.

"Personally I think we have great opportunity here to apply a bit of Triple Knot design. Three related and interdependent things: Manager needs to onboard a new employee; IT want to ensure efficient commissioning and set up for the new employee; HR need to ensure the company meeting all compliance needs. Net result -the new employee gets a good experience right from the start.

"Onboarding is often a poor experience for everyone. Getting a group together from across the business to build an overall process that works is important because this is a new employee's first impression. This could be an easy low hanging win."

Moris looked a bit puzzled. "Is that how it works? Seems a bit simple. Why isn't everyone doing it?"

Tony just smiled and cocked his head to one side.

Moris addressed the team when they resumed. "I know it got a bit tetchy earlier, but I think we should accept that there was nothing personal in it. People don't always agree, and people don't always understand each other's frustrations. In talking with Tony I think we have an opportunity here to put a small group together to look at this one thing from an across the company perspective. Perhaps a manager who does a fair bit of hiring…"

"And who doesn't always follow due process," put in Jerry.

Moris twisted around to look at Jerry. "Yes. Good idea. One of your team who knows what is needed for HR and Payroll, and Leo? One of your folk?"

"Sounds ok to me," said Leo.

"Good. You two should sponsor it and give them direction as to what is required. Perhaps get them to focus on the behaviours needed to make a good onboarding process work."

Leo and Jerry looked at each other and nodded.

Tony walked over to the to the flip chart lists and scale. "Without getting into detail right now. Given the individual conversations that we've had as well….am I right in thinking that people believe we are more Non-Adaptive than Adaptive?"

There were nods and sounds of agreement from everyone.

"Again, without going into detail today. I'd like you all to have a think about how you would know a shift has been made towards Adaptability. Moris talked about behaviours. What behaviours would you see, or hear about, that would tell you for instance that people here are more proactive than reactive?" He held his hand up. " Not right now," He said. "Just think about it so when we do have a session dedicated to defining our Adaptive behaviours then you can input to that. Right now I need to get onto understanding the rest of this Triple Knot. Specifically… the Appropriate Culture."

"Sooo… being Adaptive isn't enough?" asked Susan.

"No. It's not. It's critical that we look at the company within the context of the operating environment, and understand the type of work, type of people and expectations of our key stakeholders with regards how we look and behave.

"For example, quickfire instant management decision making that might occur in a small retail business would likely be frowned upon and quite inappropriate in a large government department always under public scrutiny. Hiring people who expect and want to work with rigid policies and procedures may not work well for an organisation that needs to shift gears rapidly and freely."

Jerry interjected, "That's one of the reasons people have given us for why they leave. Not enough support they say. I hadn't thought about it before but the recruitment pool in this city is dominated by public sector. Those experienced workers are used to having more resources around them than we are. They are also very used to having layers of decision making, which takes time, and therefore sometimes struggle with the pace needed here. That's a lightbulb moment Tony."

Tony and the others all looked thoughtful.

"Time and effort needs to be given to understanding the core behaviours that are appropriate for the company to be able to excel in the current environment. "

"We've had company values for years," jumped in Gordon. "They haven't made any difference. I think I've still got a poster on the wall in one of the workshops. That crap was a hiss and a roar and then just seemed to die."

"Hmm, I'm not surprised. I'm guessing there wasn't any updating or changing of the values as time went on?"

"Nope," grumbled Gordon. "I've even tried to get people to talk about them in meetings. No one seems interested."

"These things were fine back in the late 80s and 90s. I spent many hours myself helping businesses create their Core Values Statements. The world has moved on but sadly too many people are still peddling the old values programmes. My view is that we need to think more deeply about today's world. I'd like you to hold that thought though. It is actually one of the core Trinity Knot areas that needs working on. I do intend to spend some time with you on that but not today. Can we just spend a little more time on understanding the Appropriate Culture bit first?" Tony felt he needed to bed this area down before the team got distracted and went off in a tangent.

"It is important to recognize that what is Strategically Appropriate can change over time. Anyone here old enough to remember managers coming in to the office in walk shorts and ties?" He looked around and noticed one or too embarrassed grins. "Now imagine coming into the office looking like that now….. leaders need to consciously review and renew the set of behaviours and expectations to keep the business humming. When times, and society norms change, too many businesses have found that they have entrenched attitudes and beliefs that make it really hard to change with the times. Being sustainable means being contemporary."

Gordon shook his head, "I'm not really sure I'm getting this. Anybody else?" he asked.

There were a couple of nods.

"OK. Let me give you a real example. Some years ago I worked in a financial services company. It owned several subsidiaries that covered areas like life and health insurance, general insurance for cars and home etc as well as a very healthy managed funds investment line of products. It even owned a company who were at the top end of Trustee work, managed family trusts and executed wills etc. Quite diverse. The company was looking to get a more collective brand as they wanted to position themselves differently in the market and develop greater depth with customers and greater loyalty. You see, I could easily have my car insured but at that time I might have my family trust with another provider. I think you can see why change was a goal.

"It soon became important to rationalise as we actually had some companies competing with each other for the same customers in some product areas. There was also a lot of double up in corporate functions as each company had their own Finance, IT and HR departments.

"Now I'm really simplifying things here but a lot of work was done to understand the brand position that we wanted to establish as we had quite a range, both low cost and premium etc. Everybody still with me?"

There were nods all round and Tony could see that they were really paying attention. Stories are great he thought to himself.

"Eventually, it became evident that our main customers were people who were actually quite financially literate and who wanted to take responsibility for managing their own wealth and financial affairs.

We could see that the best place for us was to try and keep the premium product domain and try and get out of the low cost/low value areas. This meant presenting a brand that was all about you..." at this he pointed toward Susan, "....taking control of your own financial health."

"I don't quite understand yet ...." responded Susan.

"The company started marketing itself as providing products with tools that you could use online and manage things yourself. You could view your investments, change your will, levels of insurance etc. You didn't need to talk to anybody if you didn't want to. This company wasn't the cheapest but it did have higher value offerings than others. Our customers were focused on high quality and having more control.

"Simple right? The problem....and a lot of this was my team's job to try and figure out...was that we had several different companies all with their own cultures, and many of those cultures were focused around the old model of doing things *for* the customer rather than *enabling* the customer to do things for themselves. Do you understand what I'm saying?" He looked around and noticed a couple of frowns.

'Moris. You look a little puzzled."

"Ummm, I'm just processing that. You mean, originally, there were people who would understand your need from you and then fix it for you, and what you needed were people who would build things so you could fix the problems for yourself. Am I right?"

"Exactly!" affirmed Tony.

"So a feature of the Appropriate Culture for this company had to be behaviours around making things easy for others rather than perhaps making processes that only your staff could follow?" asked Jerry.

"Absolutely. Jerry you and Moris are right onto it. Now think about how would you see people behaving if they were enablers rather than fixers?" Remember this is just an example but the point is, CONTEXT will change and your culture needs to also be prepared to change as well.

"The big question for this team to answer is what does our Appropriate Culture need to look like today?"

Everyone seemed to be considering this thought.

"I can see we only have a few minutes but if I can just tie everything up a bit...The Triple Knot for a High Performance Culture is Adaptive, Appropriate and Strong. Strong is actually the easiest to understand but the most difficult to sustain.

"Once you have grappled with the need to build Adaptability, and what your culture should look like to be Appropriate for the operating context, then to make it Strong you need to make sure that your business practices and policies reinforce those behaviours. That will mean all of you being prepared to enforce and support those policies and practices because everyone else takes their lead from you."

There was silence. Everybody trying not to look at everyone else,

Finally, Moris spoke up. "That's a shitload of stuff to take in. Also, as Gordon said, we've had values statements before and at those times there was like only 4 or 5 short sentences. This looks really complex and if we start putting up statements about Adaptive elements and Appropriate ones we'll fill pages."

There was a murmur of agreement around the room.

Tony smiled. "Well, this is where I differ from a lot of my contemporaries. I'm proposing we go down quite a different route that means no slogans and big corporate statements. Yes, there is a lot to get your heads around but you don't need the whole company to bend their brains on this stuff. This is your job. You're the leadership team. I can promise you that you can do this in a way that minimises cynicism and resistance that you might get from staff. It'll also raise engagement and build greater trust. For now though, I just needed you to understand what the High Performance Culture model looks like so you can think about what the gap is between what the company currently looks like and what it could look like."

CHAPTER 7

DEEP LEADERSHIP

S usan and Gordon were having a drink in a small bar in a quiet part of town, away from the hustle and bustle of the city centre. They were both a little nervous as it felt like a date except it wasn't. After the meeting Gordon had simply asked Susan if she felt like a drink and he could drop her off home afterward as it was on his way.

"So how are you settling in Susan?" asked Gordon. "I mean you've been here for a few months and it must feel like we have a mountain to climb."

Susan shrugged, "I'm all good. You know, almost every place I've worked has had issues like we have. There's always a lot to do for management. I think it just goes with the territory now."

She frowned and leaned forward over her glass on the table, "Although….there is something that is bothering me and I …well, not really sure how to deal with it."

" I, ah…okay," uttered Gordon. He shook his head, "What is it? Can I help?"

Susan sighed heavily and squared her shoulders. She looked Gordon straight in the eye, "Well. I think there has been some dodgy finance things going on. Fraud."

"What!?" he almost shouted. Angry. "And you think it's me? Right? I'd never…"

Susan reached over and placed her hand on Gordon's arm. " I don't think it's you. In fact. I know it isn't you." Susan seemed to struggle for words for a while. Gordon sat, staring at her. Not saying anything. Just waiting for her to gather herself. She looked down and muttered, " I think it might be Moris," she whispered

"Seriously? How? Why? Moris?" Gordon was incredulous.

"I..I'm not sure," confessed Susan. "It's only. Moris was the CFO and must have seen the inconsistencies in the reporting. Maybe he was involved and let things slip through."

"Why tell me? Shouldn't you be talking to Jerry or somebody like that?" Gordon looked confused.

"To be honest. I don't really know Jerry that well. I know he is quite close with Moris. I...I feel as though I can trust you. I know I probably shouldn't be dumping something like this on you but I just didn't think I could talk to anyone else," She shook her head, "Look. Forget I mentioned it. I'm sorry. I didn't mean to talk about it today at all. I know you just wanted to have a nice drink but…."

Gordon cocked his head to one side and gazed at her as he pursed his lips. He placed his hand over hers, still resting on his arm. "No. You've done the right thing. I'm sorry. I shouldn't have gone off like that. Perhaps we can both have a think and chat tomorrow about this. Maybe think about getting Jerry involved. Those HR characters are actually quite good at this kind of thing. But don't tell him I said that. Let's have another drink and talk about something else for now. Tell me about you. I'd like to know more about Susan. The person."

She smiled, "I'd like that too."

∼

Moris was just finishing up a report to Maureen regarding the Triple Knot programme. They'd decided to call it that just between themselves for now.

There was a knock at the door and Jerry stuck his head in. "Gotta minute?"

"Jerry. Since when has HR ever taken a minute? C'mon in." He gestured to the chair by the window. "What's happening?"

Jerry made himself comfortable. "Not good news I'm afraid. Sorry, I feel I only ever bring bad news but Averil's lawyer has sent us another letter claiming that you bullied her and that they want us to go into mediation to resolve the issues."

" I wouldn't bully a fly!" blurted Moris.

Jerry held up his hand, palm outward. He nodded vigorously. "I know. I know. Don't worry. We've got this. In my experience it's often something people do when they are a bit ashamed of how they've acted. They try to justify things by diverting the blame onto others. Besides, I know this lawyer. She's a real piece of work. Once she's involved you can bet there won't be a reconciliation anywhere on the path. She's quite infamous in the ER world. She's after money.

"I've had a chat with Wiremu and we both agree that we have nothing to lose by going to mediation. We can do it without admitting any liability and it won't prejudice anything if it goes nasty and ends up in the Employment Authority. They'd probably direct us to try mediation first anyway. We of course, will respond that we will attend (if you're ok with that) and that we do not believe that there is any issue of bullying."

Moris scrunched up his nose and exhaled loudly. "OK. Let's go ahead. But why do you think she's doing this? Telling lies...there is no evidence of bullying or anything. You know that."

"Actually. I think she's doing it because she's got herself in a bit of a spot. She's after money. She lost that job she went to almost immediately. Apparently the company was on the verge of bankruptcy but didn't disclose any of that to her. It's all quite messy and I think someone may do some serious jail time."

"Bloody hell!" breathed Moris.

"Yep." Said Jerry. "Now don't you have a session with Tony today?"

"Bugger. I'm late," he grabbed his jacket as rushed out of his office.

A few minutes later Moris joined Tony at the cafe that had become their regular meeting place.

"Shit I'm really sorry Tony. I got caught up…"

"No worries. remember. You're the paying customer. Besides…" he confessed "I'm late too. I just walked in," He chuckled.

Moris ordered two coffees at the counter and sat down. He looked over at Tony, "I think the sessions with the team are going well. But we started talking about something last time and ran out of time with everything going on. Deep Leadership."

"Ahh." Tony nodded his head slowly. "Yes. I thought you might want to get into that.

Are you familiar with any of the work of Daniel Goleman?"

"The Emotional Intelligence guy?"

"Yes. That's him."

"A bit. I've read some stuff and I think it's pretty well accepted now that EI is really important."

"Yes it is. He also did a lot of work around leadership styles. Are you aware of that?"

"Can't say that I am."

"Well. He described six leadership styles. I won't go into detail on all of them but I will ask you to have a read up on them. The six styles he reckons are: Visionary; Commanding; Pacesetting; Affiliative; Democratic and Coaching."

"Okay," said Moris "Sounds interesting."

"I'll drop in some reading material for you later today. In the meantime, I have a slightly different angle to Goleman but still think his work is great.

"I don't actually see Visionary as a style. I think it is more of an attribute. The other five styles, as he calls them, are more about how you interact with people. I think Visionary is more about *what* you interact about. The others are how you operate. Anyway, that's not my point. I've taken the Goleman model and drawn it up like this…"

He pulled out his notepad and began to scribble.

Shallow

Pacesetting

Commanding

Affiliative

Democratic

Coaching

Cultivating

DEEP

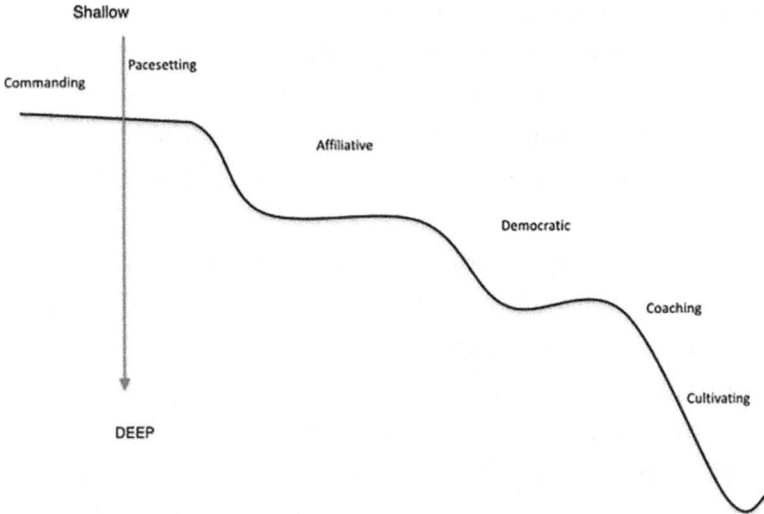

"I have a view that leadership. Real leadership, now has a new and deeper level to challenge us. For want of a better term I've labeled it 'Cultivating'."

Moris looked pensive. "I'm not really certain of what you mean. Growing things?"

Tony laughed. "Yes it is kind of. It means actively helping someone, to grow and strengthen. Improve and develop. It goes beyond coaching in my books as it means actually acting on them. Feeding them ideas, most especially, on how to become resilient"

Moris was listening carefully.

"You've heard me at times talk about shallow experience and progressing people too fast beyond their ability, and then seeing that they don't have resilience. The world of work now is moving, fast, through what I think could be described as the Societal Age," explained Tony.

"Let me try to explain like this. Sorry for the short history lesson but I think it is important in order to really grasp what is driving things today.

"The world of work over the centuries has gone through some cataclysmic changes.... I call them the 'ages of work'. I believe that there have been four most significant periods which have dictated what the world of work was like. Some people think there are more but it just depends on how granular you want to be.

"After we came out of caves and started to build communities etc, we got into what is known as the Artisan Age. Individuals became adept at a specific thing, baking, building, making pots, weaving etc. People did their thing and traded their wares pretty much from where they lived. Highly skilled specialists lived and worked out of their homes and serviced nearby communities.

"Some centuries passed and demand for goods spread, guilds and trades started to emerge and exert influence as skilled workers banded together to ensure their livelihoods as travelling merchants brought competitive goods into the communities. It was actually these merchants and commercially oriented people who drove the demand. Soon mass production of a kind started. "Eventually we entered the second major age. The Industrial Age enabled an Industrial revolution that changed the face of work forever. Manufacture became the main type of work for both artisan and non-or semi skilled workers. Factories started to spring up and cities were built around them as people flocked to work in the factories churning out goods. This age ramped up immensely with inventions of better and faster machinery. An enormous period for invention and science.

"Over time, and most especially around the turn of the 20th century business started to find greater need for administration and so large office and service based organisations began to emerge in the cities. These administrative centres demanded higher educational levels as people needed to be literate in both language and numbers. Thus the Administrative Age was developed. This Age is often overlooked but it is actually the one where we are experiencing the greatest shift now.

"People talk about the Technological Age but frankly, I think that started way back with the discovery of electricity and inventions such as radio, telephones etc. We have been in this age for a long time and it just keeps adding and changing.

"The effects of technology on the world of work is definitely cataclysmic as it has enabled faster and faster administration and allowed for instantaneous communications on a global scale.

I'm simplifying things here but I think you get the gist yes?" Moris nodded.

Tony continued. "I think we are now well into the next age, the Societal Age. Due to shifts in people's expectations about work and life and how they fit together, enabled by advances in technology, and strengthened by shifts in values around social justice and environmental resilience. "The lines between work and whole of life are now more blurred than ever and people no longer need, nor want to congregate physically to do work. There is more opportunity for people to work, where, when and how they choose. Whether we like it or not. The genie is out of the bottle. Things like pandemics have helped accelerate the whole flexible and hybrid working world.

Still with me?"

"Absolutely.." said Moris .."but I'm struggling with how this relates to Deep Leadership."

"Well. During each of the different ages there were different predominant leadership styles at play. Those leadership styles pretty much reflected the societal norms of the day and were effective in driving productivity.

"For instance, Command type leadership was exactly what brought the industrial age success. Greater affiliative and eventually more Democratic styles became the norm during the administrative and technological ages. Coaching is very much the thing now but I feel that we are needing to start developing leadership skills around an even deeper level which I call the *Cultivating* style."

Tony could see that Moris was finding this a bit difficult.

"Are you familiar with the notion of the 'mollycoddled generation'?" he asked Moris.

"No. I'm not. Is it a thing?"

"Well actually. Yes it it certainly is. For some years now research has been telling us that our younger generations are actually suffering from a culture of safetyism. In our desire to keep our kids safe we appear to have gone too far. Resilience has become a major issue. Universities are struggling for example, to find and hire enough therapists to deal with the wellness issues of students.

"Parents have become so overprotective that we aren't enabling kids to learn how to deal with challenges and stresses that they will encounter later in life. Look. This may sound like the older generation telling kids to harden up but actually this is no different from working out at the gym. Going through some physical stress helps you to become fitter and healthier. The western society has become so averse to any kind of mental stress that we have legislated even, to protect younger people from things that may cause any mental stress. We are actually doing more harm than good. Researchers are concerned about it and rightly so.

"The safetyism mindset has flowed into the workplace and organisations have even trained people around things such as 'microagression', and 'trigger warnings'. Safe spaces have been created.

"We are actively, but unwittingly, depriving our young people of the ability to develop character and mental strength."

"Wow. That sounds serious. I never thought of it like this. Touchy subject."

"Yes. It is touchy. Very touchy. But now research is really highlighting that we need to do something serious about it soon or we will have generations of anxiety ridden snowflakes unable to mentally handle anything more serious than changing a lightbulb."

Moris thought about this for a moment. "You know. Fi and I couldn't have kids so we haven't really experienced this but as you speak I've been thinking about some of our younger workers and I've seen what you are describing. But what has this got to do with Deep Leadership?"

"Well....there's a couple of things really. One is that these kids are coming into the workforce less prepared for the realities of life than they should be and so this is quite disruptive in modern workplaces when you have the complete age range of workers. Older and more worldly employees often get frustrated by the attitudes they see in younger employees.

"This easily boils over into claims of bullying, over-catastrophising and words like 'triggering' , 'toxic workplaces' etc get chucked about. Jerry will no doubt have a view on what it means for HR.

"As a leader I know the demands on my time markedly increased over the last ten years in having what I recognised as parenting conversations with employees.

"Organisations are being forced more and more to take responsibility, under legislation, to put mechanisms in place to manage wellness. Whether we like it or not, senior leaders are more and more having to fill the gaps in employees lives that they used to get from family and friends in their private lives. We need to accept that we have a place in building resilience."

"But how do you do that? Seems like they're already spoiled and it's too late. Can I say that?"

Tony chuckled. "I wouldn't necessarily say it to them but between us…fine. I believe that we need to have a leadership team who are collectively and individually prepared to allow staff to have tougher experiences, guide rather than protect them, and actually be more firm about them meeting organisational needs rather than pandering to individual expectations. The whole SLT need to feel you all have each others backs on this and are consistent in applying it."
"That simple huh?" Moris laughed

"Nope. But whoever said leadership was easy."

"My view is that we are in real danger of acting all care and little responsibility. We are pushing people into things that they have not been prepared for. It's a dangerous world for people who lack mental fitness and for the people around them. The societal pressure is heavily impacting organisational working expectations. Employees want, and expect, to progress their careers way faster than may be safe. Now I don't know what your view is but I certainly don't believe leadership is just about giving people what they say they want."

There was a pause as Tony thought about his next words. Moris looked very thoughtful indeed.

"The biggest issue I think, is that newer leaders aren't currently equipped to navigate this. Many leaders are still thinking in terms of the old paradigms. Some are thinking only in terms of newer trendy ideas like, being vulnerable. Leaders are struggling to shift at the appropriate pace and context, and situational factors are forgotten."

"How do you mean?" asked Moris

"Well, Ive noticed a lot of 'new' leaders who talk about their particular 'style'. They don't seem to understand that you need to be able to adopt, when appropriate, any number of styles. It's not about sticking to one that suits you.

"I really don't want to sound like a grumpy old guy but frankly, I think a lot of this has to do with an over reliance on woke philosophies that have little basis in reality. This might sound awful but the whole natural order for nurturing young people through development as humans has become diluted. Basic things like learning to cope with disappointment, dealing with change, actually mastering something before moving onto the next thing. Parents and grandparents used to be the main sources of help but society is such now that the parents are often just surviving themselves in the world of work and busyness. Grandparents also. Older, wiser people aren't respected and listened to. Social media is more likely to be the place where kids get their 'wisdom' from. In short, younger people are less prepared, more expectant, and less emotionally resilient."

"Everything has sped up?" suggested Moris

"Sort of. People don't take the time to check and verify a lot of what they see on their devices and they tend to react, even overreact at times. You're just as likely nowadays to develop your personal values and opinions from soundbites on social media platforms, rather than from real people, who care for you. Society has placed put more onus on workplaces to fulfil increasingly complex life demands and different expectations in workers lives. Some of this has been bolstered by legislation around responsibilities for wellbeing at work.

"But back to Deep Leadership. In the past there was more time to understand and learn new leadership capabilities. Now, there isn't time to rely on how we did things and developed leadership. We're in a new game. Remember I mentioned that some leaders are still thinking in terms of old paradigms? It's not all their fault that we have such a crisis of leadership. Many new leaders I see are very underdone and it doesn't take much for them to fail."

"I know what you mean," said Moris. "Weren't we all like that once?"

"Perhaps. But we got the edges rubbed off by mentors and people who spent deliberate time and effort on helping us learn from our experiences.

"I think leaders who are able to operate in ways that can more quickly build experience and resilience in the workforce will be the ones people want to work with. Basically, we are in real danger of burning through people if we can't shift our leaders away from output focus onto input growth. By that I mean, our leaders need to learn how to be a bigger positive influence in their employees lives rather than just their working lives. Get deeper, really use the Emotional Intelligence to know the aspirations, challenges, and lives of your workers."

Tony picked up his empty cup and stared into it.

"I feel like I've just made a bit of a speech but I have seen so many talented people come a cropper because their mix of expectations and opportunities have put them into roles they simply aren't psychologically resilient or mature enough to do well and this flows down through the organisation ranks."

"Wow." Moris paused. Thinking it through a little. "I understand what you're saying but how the hell do you actually do it?"

Tony looked straight at Moris and said. "A mix of an Employment Value Triple Knot and a leadership team who can cope with sometimes being unpopular with staff, focus on building their staff's resilience and building them into mature adults. Acting a bit more like responsible parents by saying no when it is the right thing to do. Not giving in to entitled pleading. Allowing people to make mistakes and helping them learn from those. Dealing quickly with poor behaviours and being there to mentor when needed. Don't rush them into leadership roles and above all, don't let them rush you into putting them into leadership roles. *Cultivating* people."

"Sounds easy," joked Moris.

"Sure," said Tony. "Any parent will tell you it's the easiest job in the world….not."

CHAPTER 8

THE WORKPLACE TRIPLE KNOT

L eo and Jerry were discussing who should be on the Onboarding Team and how they'd make it work. They had decided to include Mara, the HR co-ordinator, Prabash from IT, and Sarah, a team leader from Gordon's group. She was one of the worst for not following procedure.

After deciding on the brief to give the team Leo and Jerry were having a coffee in the cafeteria. Leo looked at Jerry and said. "Do you remember my mate Darren? You met him at a barbie at mine a while back."

"The crazy Glaswegian?"

"Yes that's him. He calls you the Coroner...Human Remains expert. Ha!"

"Exactly what I'd expect from someone from Glasgow. I seem to remember he said his grandad was from the Gorbals. He'd know all about bodies then. Good though. I kinda like it. The Coroner....I might keep that handle. My Superhero alter-ego."

"Anyway. He suggested I talk to you about my concerns around this stuff that Tony Delahunt is doing with us."

"Concerns? You haven't said anything at the meetings."

"No I haven't. That's mainly because I feel that a lot of this stuff is going right past me. It's that HR kinda stuff that you like. I just don't get all the triple ring stuff."

"Triple Knot."

"Yeah. That too. I mean….we need to improve. We all know that. And we need to work better together. Why doesn't Moris just take control and tell us what he wants from us? He's the boss after all."

Jerry looked at Leo and said " Do you really believe that'll work best?"

"I know it will work best," said Leo "That's how we did things in South Africa. I mean, what is the point of being the boss if you can't tell people what you expect to achieve and hold them accountable?"

Jerry ballooned his cheeks and blew a long slow breath out. "C'mon Leo. I really think you might need to accept that South Africa has a very different work culture than here. Or at least it did. Things have changed all over the world in how managers and leaders operate. Have you done much reading on this? I'm not trying to be clever but management and leadership are both whole areas of major research into why organisations succeed or fail. The old command and control style of leadership has largely disappeared these days."

"Well it shouldn't have," said Leo, "it worked."

"Perhaps it did. But time has moved on and so have expectations of workers, not to mention employment legislation etc. Command and control may have been appropriate for some contexts but certainly not all. Not in this country, and not in most from everything I've read. I'm sure you really don't want Moris telling you what to do. I know you value your autonomy to make decisions in your space. Why would you think others don't feel the same and want autonomy in their jobs?"

"Ok, Ok. I'm never going to win this argument but surely there is a need sometimes for a bit of command and control? You know, when we have a serious need to improve?"

"Yes there is Leo. But it's the same for the other leadership styles, democratic, affiliative etc. You need to understand which style to adopt for any given time. It can't always be the same."

"I never thought of it that way. That's a good question. How do you know which is the best style for any particular time?"

"My view is that the answer to that very much depends on the judgement of your leaders. It is something we need to agree as a team. Otherwise we end up confusing our staff as to what acceptable behaviours are. We need to be consistent in our approach. One thing that I'm not sure of for instance though is whether or not the entire leadership team actually knows anything about the different styles, let alone think about how to decide which is appropriate for different contexts. I think I'll bring it up at our next meeting with Tony."

"I'm still not sure though of the value of this Triple Knot design. I hear everything that he has told us and it seems to make sense at the time but I need more. Can you help translate this into language I can understand better? Plus I just can't figure out how to use what I know."

Jerry grinned, "Sure I can. But the quality of my advice will largely depend on the conduciveness of the environment in which I give it and on the motivational energy I can apply given the long day I've had. That's a Triple Knot right there that says —Let's start over a Bushmills after work. Your shout."

"I think I'm already beginning to understand," grumbled Leo.

∿

"Hi everyone. Before we get into things I just want to check on how you are all feeling about what we are doing and where it is all taking us. I think it's critical that we are all on the same page about this and if we aren't then we do need to have more conversations so that we can clarify and understand all of the implications. As you know, I've been spending a bit of time one on one with Tony and I've found it really helpful in building a greater understanding of all the different aspects of what we have been discussing."

Moris looked around the room and saw expectant faces. He did notice both Gordon and Susan quickly glance at each other with what seemed to be frowns?

"Susan? Gordon? You both looked as though you may have some questions?"

"No," they both said almost in harmony. "I mean," added Gordon. "No questions from me. Susan?"

"None here," she said. Moris thought she looked a little uncomfortable.

"Are you sure?" he asked. "You don't sound too convincing."

Susan waved her hand and smiled. "No. All good here. My mind was on other work things."

Moris paused a moment, then nodded. "Allright. It's really important that we try to focus now. I need to be sure that we are all looking at the same picture."

He looked about the room and waited. Leo took out his mobile phone and turned it off. He put it on the table in front of him and looked at the others. They all did the same.

"Fantastic," declared Moris "So. I wanted to spend a bit of time reminding us of what we have covered so far and have space to air any questions or comments in order to help get a shared understanding. Please feel free to chime in if I miss anything or you think of something that could help. Also, ask questions and/or offer answers if you want. Tony has suggested that I lead this session and he will chip in if I'm on the wrong wavelength. He's also suggested that it would be even better if any of you jump in before him. So to make this work I'll go to Tony if no one else has spoken up first and we need something made clearer. How does that sound?"

There was a general murmur of agreement and so Moris got into it. "To recap then…Over the last month we've had several sessions around the future and how we can develop our strategy moving forward.

"The retreat that we held over a couple of days allowed us some time to look at the key challenges facing us and the strengths and weaknesses we have. We also discussed the environment which we operate within and considered what the implications for the company were. I think there was general consensus that we pretty much needed to spend more time and energy on a reset of the business model and try to develop a stronger performance orientation across the board."

He paused and looked around. Everyone seemed attentive.

"We've since then had a couple of SLT meetings with Tony presenting some new concepts for us to think about. Now this is where I might need some help…We talked about a concept called the Triple Knot. Tony drew diagrams up on the board which I'm not even going to attempt because even though it looks simple, it would easily explain why I didn't get any awards for art in school."

At this there were several chuckles.

"The Triple Knot symbolises the relationship and interdependence of any three things. To be perfectly honest I still struggle a little with how to know what three things could go in the circles. Anyone?"

Leo looked over at Jerry and nodded. "I'll take this. Jerry and I have been grappling a bit with this as well. I have to admit, it took me a while for it to click. Here's how I see it. The three things are related in a way that you can't have any of them existing effectively without the other two." He looked at the team. "And… if you work on one area, it will have a real impact on the other two. So the idea is to try and think about coming up with things that will have a good impact on all three.Yeah?"

Moris sat back a little in his chair at that.

Leo continued ,"An obvious example.. was the example that we used. Birth, life, death. You can't give birth without first having life. You can't have a life without being born and you can't die, if you haven't had life. Something like that anyway. I know scientifically some might argue but it's a simple analogy."

Jerry jumped in. "In a worksense example, work, pay, employment. You won't get employed if there is no work. You won't get paid if you aren't employed. And you won't work if there is no pay," Jerry continued, " I know it seems simplistic and if you really wanted to you could intellectualise arguments around this concept but from a pragmatic perspective, I totally get it. "Remember we talked about a Triple Knot for Economic, Societal, and Workforce Sustainability? Quite simply the three are related as you wouldn't have the money to invest in your workforce if you didn't look after the needs of your customers and shareholders (Societal)."

There was silence. Everyone considering Jerry's words.

"I think I see it now," Susan declared. " You can make this thing as complicated as you like but keeping it simple allows you to dive down into how three elements relate so that making any decisions about one of them you need to consider how it will affect the other two. Right? It's just a way of focusing your thinking a bit more."

Moris looked over toward Tony and pointed at Susan. "Bang on Susan. I think some of us have been looking for the deep and meaningful secrets in this when in fact it is just a tool for helping us to align our thinking around things." Tony was nodding and holding both thumbs up.

Jerry was looking over at Gordon. "I'm not sure Gordon is totally comfortable yet. Am I right Gordon?"

"No. Actually. I'm just processing it a bit and thinking of it in application. I can see how it works with the economic health and all that but how do you use it to make the business better? Tony talked about using it as a design tool"

Moris stood up and picked up a whiteboard pen.

"As I say, I've been working more with Tony and part of that has been to help me stay ahead of things as they relate to this. Can I try and show you something that Tony and I chucked around recently?"

"You've got the pen," said Jerry with a smile.

"I think I'll ask Tony to draw up a Triple Knot while I talk. OK Tony?"

Tony smiled wryly as he took the proffered whiteboard pen. He went to the board and began to draw as Moris started to speak.

"We talked about the Triple Knot relationship between the organisational sustainability indicators. We talked about the Triple Knot relationship with three aspects of culture: Adaptive; Appropriate; and Strong. There are things we can discuss and build plans around in each of these that should result in positive change. I know that Jerry and his team have been giving the High Performance Culture quite a bit of thought.

"There are a few more critical Triple Knots that we should think about first though and Tony and I have discussed a Triple Knot that we think is perhaps more fundamental to understand, in this day and age, than the other Triple Knots if we are to seriously redesign how we work."

He stepped back toward the flipchart stand where Tony had produced a completely new diagram.

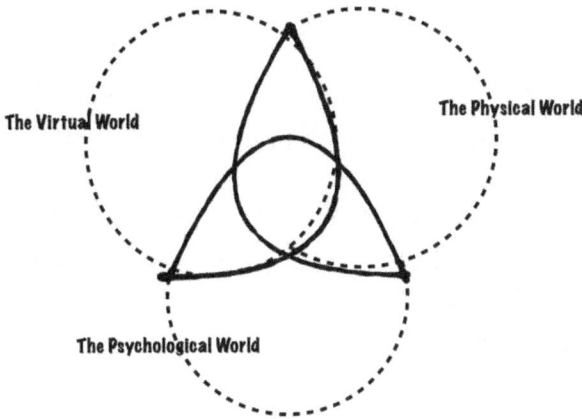

"This is the Workplace Triple Knot. Some of us can remember a time when the world seemed less complicated. Life revolved around your home and family life and, for most, your working life was the other bit. It wasn't like they never intersected. They did. For some, much more often than was comfortable. But overall, you could apply your conscious self to wherever you were and whatever you were doing. People talked about personal life and work as two different worlds.

"Nowadays we all live and work in three different worlds. This is shown as the three dotted circles. For an employer, we need to think about all three of these environments and try and understand how we impact on a person's overall life both where they intersect and overlap. Think about Health and safety, now also wellbeing. When we design a physical work environment, do we think about making sure it's safe? Of course we do. But what about the virtual, slash, digital world? Apart from the usual cyber security practices, do we look at how we can keep our staff safe? Or do we just look to minimise potential damage to the company?

"The hardest one for me to get my head around is the psychological world. You can't see it, everyone's is different, and not many businesses have people equipped to help if there is a problem."

"Yes. And I have to say people are a lot less resilient nowadays with regards what they call 'unsafe'. What's real and what's imagined is harder to establish. Makes it really difficult for an employer," suggested Jerry.

Moris was thoughtful, "Exactly. Nowadays I hear a lot more about the responsibility of the organisation towards it's employees. What is real and what is expected.

"Now you can see inside the wider work/life bubbles, a Triple Knot. That's what we have to think about when we are designing the operating model. How do we reconcile our boundaries? Especially when people are working from home or anywhere. At anytime." He pointed up to the Flipchart drawing, "As a company, how much are we accountable for in terms of making sure they are safe in all three work environments? Also, how does the ' Work' Triple Knot affect the 'Life' Triple Knot? "

"Wow. That's a really tricky question," said Gordon. "Way bigger than just keeping the heaters on in the workshop and having a health and safety committee."

Moris continued "I don't want to make things bigger than Ben Hur but I was thinking this isn't just limited to our workforce. It applies to our customers and the communities within which we operate. How we interact with them. How we deliver to them…what impact do we have on their worlds?"

He let that sink in for a few moments. "But I think one step at a time, eh? I feel like we are now discussing deeper things than we were a month ago but I just want to check again that we are all still in synch. I don't want you to say all good if you aren't. Once we have gained more understanding of these concepts we have to try and pull together a comprehensive narrative to describe a revitalised, contemporary and sustainable organisation for the Board to get excited by."

Moris waited for any response but everyone looked comfortable. Eager even. Moris exuded confidence as he continued.

"So the plan from here is that we have one more team session with Tony here around the Triple Knot design concept next week and then we will have a two day retreat at which I would like us to pull it together into something more like an actual plan, or roadmap, for delivery to the board. The two day retreat is one month from now and I expect all of you to contribute to the proceedings."

Jerry liked the direct approach that Moris had adopted here.

"There are some things in train already but I'd be really keen for specific 'owners' to present proposed ways forward. We can discuss details a bit later but …let me see if I have this right. Susan and Jerry are working on the organisational sustainability Triple Knot. Especially the metrics. Yes?"

Susan looked at Jerry and they both nodded.

"Jerry and his team are looking at the High Performance Culture Triple knot." Again there were nods.

"Gordon and Leo. I would really like you two to explore the Workplaces Triple Knot please. You will need of course to involve Jerry and Susan but if you two could own it that would be great. Okay?"

"Sounds like a plan," said Leo. "No problem," added Gordon.

"Tony is on call for any of you to bounce things off if you want to. I'll see you all together next week."

"Ahh. What about you?" chimed Jerry. "Are you doing something for the retreat as well?"

"Yes. I'm going to dive into Deep Leadership."

CHAPTER 9

CONTEMPORARY CULTURE

Jerry and his team were sitting in a small but comfortable conference room at a local hotel. It was an away day for the team of six to focus on the High Performance Culture and start to develop up ideas on how to make it a reality.

He'd decided not to use a facilitator for this meeting as it was important that his team had a chance to try and understand the major concepts being talked about with the SLT.

Jerry was explaining the High Performance Culture Triple Knot and unfortunately was getting frustrated by Shona, his OD advisor.

"I don't like this stuff at all. I think it lacks real modern research behind it and hasn't been through any real sort of academic rigour," pronounced Shona with her usual air of superiority.

Jerry took a deep breath, loudly, through his nostrils. As he looked at the others in the room all rolling their eyes at Shona's remark. She didn't seem to notice.

Before he could respond, his Senior HR Advisor, Brian, held up his hand. "Can I get this?" he asked, looking at Jerry, who nodded.

"Shona. When Jerry first told us about this I picked up a copy of the book. *'Corporate Culture and Performance'*. Have you read it?"

"No. I haven't," she said. "Why would I read something that isn't up with the times? That book is so old now."

"So what has age got to do with it? Tell me. Do you disagree that culture should be Adaptive, Appropriate and Strong?"

"Well no. But the ideas are dated and we need to be contemporary."

"Firstly…what would that look like? Secondly…how do you know the ideas are dated if you haven't read the book?" asked Brian

"The new culture would need to reflect society more closely and be very diverse and inclusive. That wouldn't have been the case back then," said Shona.

" Well. You and I can argue DEI later but what you saying is it would need to be *Appropriate* to the modern context?"

"Well….yes," Shona responded, a little less bombastically.

Jerry was quietly enjoying this.

"And what if things change in the context?" questioned Brian. "What then?"

"Well we would need to watch for that and change as well," came the haughty response.

"Hmmm, sounds like we'd need to be *Adaptive*…." mused Brian.

Jerry was really enjoying this now.

Shona was looking daggers at Brian.

"Seems to me that those old Harvard Professors might have got something right," commented Brian, looking unfazed at Shona's demeanour.

Shona didn't say anything. Just turned and stared out of the window tight lipped.

"I think morning tea has just arrived," announced Mara.

"Ok. Let's have a break for about 15," said Jerry

Morning tea was in a a larger reception area outside of the conference room.

Jerry walked over to Brian and said under his breath, "Nicely done. I'm impressed."

"Ah. No problem. She just annoys me. A real 'holier than thou' and superior 'I have a PhD' manner. I hate that kinda crap."

Jerry chuckled, "Me too." He tilted his head sideways and glanced at Brian. "Did you really read all of that book?" he asked

"Of course I did," said Brian through a mouthful of scone. "About twenty years ago."

Jerry nearly choked laughing.

After morning tea, everyone filed back into the conference room and took their seats.

"Right," said Jerry. What we are needing to do is figure out how we become a High Performance Culture and pull together a high level plan for me to present to the exec team next month."

"Next Month!" exclaimed HR advisor Amy. "That gives us no time to run an engagement survey to get staff views. We haven't done one in a while. Then we need to pull together some interested staff to start working on a plan to work on the things to improve…" she tailed off as she noticed Jerry shaking his head.

"No," he said. " We need to build something now, at a reasonably high level, but enough to go to the board for them to consider. Remember this culture change programme is one part of a number of things we need to look at as an organisation."

"Then we should at least go and get a recognised company to come in and do an assessment of our current culture so we can get an accurate view of what we need to focus on to get to this High Performance Culture. Whoever we get needs to be qualified psychs and have a tool ready to go."

"Hold on. Hold on. We aren't going that deep yet. We just need to develop a high level plan. A roadmap. Also, I'm very leery of engagement surveys and 'Culture Assessment' tools. I would rather we got clear on some higher level things first. For example, our principles around managing change. One of which might be around how we involve our people in this.

"I'd also like to suggest that an 'engagement survey' is not that helpful in assessing culture. We can argue that out a bit later if you want but I agree that we will need to grapple with understanding our current culture against what our 'desired' culture looks like. There is still a lot of work to be done on defining that. Until we are comfortable that we know what that might look like I don't want anybody from an external consultancy anywhere near this. They tend to try and sell you on their view of what your culture should look like."

Brian piped up,

"Dead right. I remember working for a company once who brought in this outfit who had a whole programme about 'Becoming Blue". They'd colour coded everything and assessed the business to see if it was green or red or yellow or….something. The ideal was Blue. Staff called it 'Project Smurf' and all I could think of was sadness. Why on earth would you want to be blue?"

Mara giggled. "That's funny," she said

Everyone (except Shona) smiled.

"Qian. You haven't said much today. What are your thoughts?"

Qian was relatively new to the organisation having started straight out of university with a degree in HR. She'd only been with the business for around 4 months but was already showing real promise as an HR Advisor.

"This is all quite new to me and I think very exciting. I'm still learning but I think it is really good that we are being given this chance to design something for ourselves. We might get some things wrong but that's how we learn isn't it?"

"Very wise," said Jerry "I agree. We have an opportunity here to not only build a roadmap but to actually provide some real input into what the company culture should be." He looked about the room. "My view is that as the expert team that the rest of the business is looking to, we should at least put forward a view as to what we think the appropriate culture for this company might look like. I know these things aren't generally done this way but we should be close enough to knowing the business to be able to suggest what sort of behaviours will help us succeed in today's world."

Qian raised her hand to ask a question, " Can we please spend more time on understanding the Adaptive Culture first? I mean, from what you've shown us it seems reasonably straightforward but how do we actually know we've got there? I'd feel a lot more confident about creating a view of the Appropriate Culture if we could dig a bit more into the already defined Adaptive Culture elements to a level of detail more useful to us."

"That's a great idea Qian. Let's spend some time doing that and see how it develops."

"Hmmph. This isn't very scientific," uttered Shona.

"Since when was culture scientific?" responded Brian.

At that, Jerry went over the whiteboard and started to write. Across the top he wrote the heading "Adaptive Culture" and then under that he drew a vertical line dissecting the board into two columns. He then headed one column ' ELEMENT" and the other column 'BEHAVIOURS WE WOULD SEE'

"Right. Let's brainstorm," he said as he wrote under the first the heading -Bureaucratic versus Entrepreneurial.

ADAPTIVE CULTURE	
ELEMENT	BEHAVIOURS WE WOULD SEE
- Bureaucratic/Entrepreneurial	

"I'd like you all to think about what would you actually see people doing that suggests they are being entrepreneurial. I know it's hard but think about if you were to describe, say…me as being an entrepreneur, then how would that go? What would you say to someone? Write some ideas down and we'll do the same for the other elements. Later, we can look at what kind of behaviours do we actually currently observe and experience here that might describe bureaucratic thinking. We can do this for each of the elements until we have useful list of behaviours that describe what our aspiration versus what we currently have might look like."

"I like that but it might mean we end up with a fairly big list," suggested Mara

"Well, let's see what we end up with and likely we can look at a process of trimming down later on. Remember, we are brainstorming so we should try to just generate ideas first and we can refine things afterward. All good?"

Jerry scanned the faces in the room, and once again, with the exception of Shona, everyone looked happy to move on.

After about an hour the group were quite pleased with themselves as they had created a large list of items. Jerry suggested that they park it for now and come back to it a bit later. He wanted to look more at the organisation's 'Appropriate Culture' question first.

"So Qian. You suggested that in looking more at the Adaptive culture we might get more understanding in how to define the Appropriate Culture. Has this worked for you?"

" I think so," said Qian. "It's given me more of an idea on how we might think about culture."

Jerry looked about at the team again and said, "How does everyone else feel?"

"Well. I have to be honest and I'm still uncomfortable with where this might be taking us. It just doesn't fit with everything I've learned about organisational culture and how to develop it," said Shona. This time, seemingly with a little more humility than her other contributions to date.

"Ok" said Jerry. "I'd sort of anticipated that this subject would be one that we would struggle with. So, I asked Tony Delahunt to join us for lunch and afterward to give us his view around this subject based on his vast experience and success in working with organisations in this very space. I suggest we break now and people can check email and stuff and then lunch is just outside in the reception room where we had morning tea. Tony should be arriving soon."

~

"I'm not sure I can quite see what you mean," uttered Gordon as he looked over Susan's shoulder at the screen in front of them. They were looking at a spreadsheet showing a list of invoices paid over a month. It was two month's old.

"Ok. Now look," suggested Susan as she showed the same page

but this time with highlighted lines through it. There were five rows highlighted throughout the spreadsheet and they were all spread right across the month.

"What do you see now?" she asked.

"Well noth…" he tailed off. "Oh. I see." Each line item was for a different purchase and from a different supplier. But each item had the same bank account number.

"Ouch!" exclaimed Gordon. "You're right. It does look like something fishy going on here. What do you think we should do?"

"Wait. There's more," whispered Susan. "I've found that this has been going on for around 5 months. I can't see anything earlier than that and it all seemed to stop a few weeks ago."

She dipped into her desk drawer. "I printed these off this morning." They were copies of the original invoices and all were signed off with the same signature. Moris A. Bak.

"Holy shit," Gordon breathed. "We've gotta talk to Jerry."

"You know him better than I do. Should we?"

Gordon thought for a moment. "Yes. I don't see what else we can do. He's a straight up bloke. I think he'll keep it confidential and he'll know what to do."

"So do you want to talk to him or should I?"

Gordon paced over to the window and stared out at the park below.. " Actually. I think we should do this together. I don't think it is fair on you and I think if Jerry knows that we are both in support of each other it lends weight to getting it sorted."

Susan bit her lip and looked over at Gordon.

"Alright. If you think that's the best thing to do." She sighed deeply. "It's a damn shame. I actually quite like Moris. As…as a boss I mean," she added hurriedly.

"It seems such a silly thing to do when everything is in front of him. I actually thought we were getting somewhere with the redesign and reset of the business as well."

"Yeah. I thought so as well. Also I've known Moris for years. This just isn't him." He sucked in a huge breath, "I guess you can never really know a person eh?" sighed Gordon.

~

Leo was meeting for lunch with his friend Darren at a cafe just around the corner from the office. "I took your advice and spoke to the Coroner," said Leo.

Darren grinned at him and winked. "Sa wha' did yer wee man say?" he drawled.

"Actually. Good advice. Even from and HR man. I think I'm starting to understand this stuff now as well. I don't know why I struggled before as the basic ideas are pretty straightforward. I think I was trying to see much more in it than there is. It's actually quite good and I've found myself thinking about it more and more. I'm finding it quite helpful in trying to design better processes with my team"

"Is it like some kinda Agile thing or sommin?"

"No.No. Nothing like that. It's really just a way of thinking about things so you end up with not creating more issues somewhere else when you solve one in front of you."

"You mean it's like the auld wicked problem stuff?"

"Well , not quite but it could be used to help in that as well. Let me show you." Leo grabbed a napkin and started to draw.

"Tha's a wee Celtic Knot!" exclaimed Darren. "A've got one tattooed on mi shooder."

"I'know," laughed Leo.

"This is the core idea. Triple Knot thinking. Basically, the relationship of three things..."

"Aye. Ah ken this. Ah am a Scot yi know." So that's what he's banging on aboot? We'll have kulcha in ye afore ye know it."

Leo laughed again. "It's a really useful model for helping us to redesign things. Gordon and I are using it to try and understand how different work environments can work better together for our staff. I mean... there is a physical workplace, you know, the office for example, and a virtual workplace, online in cyberspace, and one that we hadn't really thought about. The psychological workplace."

As he talked he wrote this on the digram to illustrate the connection.

"Wheel look at you!" Darren sat back in his chair "Gettin all yaldi on me!"

"I'm not even going to pretend you used a real word there" said Leo grinning.

"Anyway. We're looking at how we can make all three safer for staff when we design things."

Darren held up his hands "Ok. Now food's here. Haud yer wheesht and let's eat."

Leo frowned and looked at Darren. "Are you ever going to learn to speak English?" he joked.

Darren grinned and shook his head.

CHAPTER 10

CHANGING THE PARADIGM

I t was now 1:30pm and lunch had been very tasty. The HR team were ready to go back into the room, or as Jerry was feeling, the arena. Shona's attitude had somewhat soured the day but now Tony had joined the group and hopefully things should get better from there.

Jerry introduced Tony.

"I'd like to introduce you all properly to Tony Delahunt. You've all been aware that he has been working with the senior team and more specifically, with Moris, as his executive coach.

Tony has had a long career across a number of organisations in both the public and private sectors. He has operated at CEO level and as a private consultant has been internationally recognised as a thought leader in the development of organisational culture and leadership."

Jerry turned his gaze toward Shona and observed her reaction to this. She was staring at the wall on the other side of the room.

"Tony has developed some concepts around building and sustaining High Performance Organisations and most especially with a focus on workforce sustainability. He has real, practical experience in workplace change having been the executive leader for transformation in twelve different organisations. He has worked in hi-tech, science and research, financial services, education, health and several public sector entities.

"We've been lucky to secure Tony's assistance in redesigning our business to be more contemporary and sustainable. I can't think of a better person to do this. I've asked him along today to give us a bit of a view as to the concepts he has been working with us on and help answer any questions you might have. Hopefully this will give us a real boost in our core area of responsibility, which is to help the organisation to design and implement a more sustainable, performance culture. Tony. We're all yours."

Tony stepped up toward the board. "Thanks Jerry. I know you are all probably a little nervous as to what I might say today. Hopefully, I will say something of interest to you and not bore you completely. Please just make me aware if it isn't working for you and/or if you have any questions. I'd much prefer this to be a conversation rather than a performance.

"First though, I'd like to get something out of the way. I am aware that some of you have come into your roles after recently completing academic studies. I'm not going to tell you what the books say. I'm not going to give you any recipes for success. You've already seen some of those.

"Some of what I say therefore will be quite new to you as it isn't in any academic programme. In fact, you may think that some ideas are reckless, with lack of academic verification. That's ok. As long as you…" and at this he pointed to everyone in the room. "…keep an open mind and understand that business tends to move much faster than academia in coming up with new ideas to improve. Basically, you don't have the luxury of time to conduct surveys and gather data. If you don't act, your competitors can get too far ahead of you.

"Many organisations will only do what the professors say is good to do based on the research that they have been doing into great companies. You've only got to look at books like Good to Great and Built to Last. Excellent material, but somewhat after the companies who were in those studies, had already been innovating and changing. Or not, in the case of those who failed. I, well, I come from the angle of trying to create businesses that Universities wish to study.

"The thing though that I want you to keep in mind is that my concepts, as described, are different from what the established beliefs may be. They won't be things you have seen before. But that doesn't mean they won't work. In some way or other, I have been using and refining these ideas for at least 35 years in every organisation I've worked with. I just want you to put on your logic hat and open your reasoning mind and listen and try and understand from that perspective.

"Any questions before I start to sound like a university lecturer?" Tony looked at each face and then smiled. "Having said that, I have a few slides to help the conversation…"

Tony started his slide show. The first slide was a collection of pictures of people working, by themselves, in groups, in factories, and in offices.

"As I said…please just jump in and ask questions or make comments whenever you like."

He paused a moment and then began.

"Over the centuries, the nature of working life has changed. It will aways continue to do so.

"There have been times though where those changes have been more profound and perhaps more revolutionary than the expected gradual evolution processes. The more profound shifts haven't all happened in big bangs but they are clearly recognisable as events."
Tony's slides showed a timeline of different eras of work.

"The shift from local craftsman and artisan work. Often done in the home, to the establishment of factory production. That took several hundreds of years but was a fundamental shift in work. Of course we have all heard of the Industrial Revolution. That really changed the game as huge factories set up and whole cities formed around them as large numbers of workers spent their time inside buildings working machinery.

"Then came what I call the Administration Revolution where business needed to be more formalised, rules and regulations took hold and the workforce needed more literate and skilled administrators.

Offices grew to meet the skylines and we lived in an age of the nine to five clerical worker.

"In the last few decades we've had an Information Technology Revolution and that is still going as things such as AI really change work. Instantaneous mobile communication and access to secure information via technology mean that geographical boundaries are no longer limiting factors. The nine to five era is basically over.

"Changed worker expectations, social norms and behaviours, and social media use have been driving another tectonic shift. Societal Revolution. There is almost complete blurring of work and other life aspects. High social conscience driving industry policies. Environmental factors to be considered etc. Mostly though it is showing as the work anywhere, anytime revolution. Whole offices are empty as people work from home and make the work fit their other interests rather than the other way around.

"All still with me?" He glanced around and saw that everyone was listening closely.

"Each of these different work eras have demanded various predominant styles of management and leadership. Different workforce skill levels and capabilities.

"All of these different work eras had different organisational cultures. All of them consistent with the times they were in. Organisational cultures have pretty much always , to a large degree, reflected societal culture of the day. It isn't a new phenomenon as some 'experts' seem to suggest.

"The thing is though, very little attention was given to the deliberate development and management of culture. It just happened. Over the latter half of the last century leaders began to understand a great deal more about the impact of culture on business. Most especially as major shifts in western society (at least) began to emphasise individual rights and equality. The civil rights movements, supported by increasingly socially conscious generations encouraged a greater focus on how people thought and behaved and what values should be reinforced.

"Smart organisations began to recognise the impact and power of company culture as a major force in achieving and sustaining performance. In the 1970's, 80's and 90's especially, a lot of management focus was on understanding and growing strong cultures. There was a very strong belief that culture was the difference. There was almost a pandemic of culture going on."

Tony looked over toward Shona. "That's the era when Organisational Development really became a thing and was introduced into mainstream business."

"Researchers from the major universities produced papers and books covering the subject of culture and even though some were way off track there were several useful books that anybody in the business of organisation change and culture work should ensure they are familiar with as they really set the tone for future thinkers. Two I would very strongly suggest are 'Corporate Culture and Performance' by John Kotter and James Heskett of Harvard University, and 'The Living Company' by Arie De Geus, former head of Royal and Dutch Shell's Strategic Planning Group."

Shona held up her hand and Tony nodded toward her. "Aren't those books a little out of date now though?" she asked.

Tony gave a short laugh and answered, "Yes they have been around a while," he cocked his head to one side. "But why should that matter? No research since then….. and there has been a hell of a lot. Has suggested that the concepts within those books, among some others, is wrong. In fact pretty much all research since then heavily supports the concepts those authors expressed.

"Also, you have to remember that these books talk about the 'what' and 'why'. Not the 'how' . That is something that really does need to be contemporary."

"I don't quite follow you," huffed Shona.

"Let me try this then. Would you agree that popular music is a big factor in youth culture?"

"Yes of course it is," said Shona. "Everyone knows that."

"Do you think that was any different in the 50's, 60's or 70's? Or for that matter, in the 1920's?"

Shona sat silently chewing on her bottom lip.

"Music has been a consistent element in defining youth culture for a very long time. He held up a finger. Let's call that '*the What*'." He held up a second finger. " Now '*The Why*'. Because it resonates with how youth feel about the world and brings them together as a point of shared interest. It's also a statement of identity and rebellion against the old establishment.

"That has always been the case. Youth in the 1950s listened to Rock and Roll rather than jazz or orchestral music. In the 60's and 70's it was electric blues and then many different streams of rock. Mostly in protest to the 'establishment'. Think about how music surrounded the hippie culture and its association with free speech and civil rights. In Britain there was the Mods and the Rockers. A shift away from the recent wartime lifestyle of the previous generation.

"Nowadays…well, music is still important but it is a different shape than before. What's different? Context. The environment. Electronics changed that in the 50s and the digital revolution has had a huge effect nowadays. Ultimately though, people are still much as they have been for thousands of years."

"I disagree. Values are different now," proclaimed Shona.

"How so?"

"Well, for one thing. People are more environmentally conscious than previous generations. Also they are much more socially conscious and fair than the past."

"I'm sorry Shona but those aren't different values. They are simply reflective of the current context. The underlying values of wanting to be fair and just, and of wanting to protect the world from bad things have always been there. The fact that in the past people were largely ignorant of human impacts on the environment doesn't mean they wouldn't have tried to protect the environment as they are now. I strongly suspect that had we the knowledge that we have today then things would be quite different.

"Looking around at the state of the world today I wouldn't agree that people are any more fair or just than at any other time in history.

People are no more or less virtuous than those of the past. Yet every generation thinks they are better than the ones before them. In fact, if you look at the evidence, rather than the media, you'll find pretty much all of the negative statstics are getting worse. Not better."

Shona looked a little chastened at that revelation.

"Look. We see a lot of stuff on the net about Baby Boomers and Gen Z and Millenials etc as well. People are people. As an OD person I'm sure you can appreciate the value of evidence and data. Do you know that there is absolutely zero evidence to support the claims that different generations can be stereotyped in the manner that popular media suggest? Actually the opposite. Serious academic research into the generations has found most of the 'accepted' myths to be simply that. Myths. You need to look deeper. Marketers don't. They have a story to sell and however shallow it is, in today's world people lack the time or the inclination to actually get beyond what is put in front of them. It sells.

"Sorry everyone. Enough of me preaching. But I do want to make a very important point.The context for the world of work (and life) changes. Sometimes it changes more profoundly than at other times. Yet we tend to continue to try and do the things we have done in the same way and with the same tools. This is a recipe for failure. We need to adjust how we approach things to be more attuned to the context."

"Can I suggest we have a short break?" suggested Brian.

"Sure," said Jerry. "Let's take just 10 minutes and reconvene."

Jerry went over to talk with Tony whilst everyone went out of the room for some fresh air.

"I've got issues with that one." He murmured so no one else but Tony would hear.

"I know what you mean. To be honest though, she's only saying what her training has embedded in her. She is very typical of today's 'experts' in organisation culture. Maybe it's old age but I do worry that there are a lot of people in this area of work who can't think any more deeply than what the magazines and their professors tell them. I know I'm cynical but it's 'easy money' for a lot of people who just promote popular ideas. Most of them have never actually been in the arena and they don't speak from experience at all. What would you like me to do? I might be being unkind but I don't think she wants to acknowledge that other ideas may be valid."

"She is going to be either a terrorist or a great supporter. This is really her 'aha!' moment right in front of her. I would like you to push on with your presentation and let her decide for herself. I don't think you need to convince her of anything. If I need to address her as an issue later on I will. This is too important to allow it to fall into the snake oil vat."

Tony grinned. "OK. Why don't we get em back in."

CHAPTER 11

CULTIVATING LEADERSHIP

Moris and Maureen had just finished going over the Board report and they were both quite pleased. Staff turnover had dropped a couple of percent in the last two months and even though it was way too early to celebrate success it set a positive mood.

They both agreed that it was likely due to the leadership team consciously behaving a little more as a team than before and it was starting to rub off on the middle managers who unconsciously were passing on a better vibe to staff.

"Do you think this is Tony's influence?" asked Maureen

"I do," said Moris. "But to be fair, the guys have really stepped up. I note they are being more thoughtful and deliberate in how they communicate with each other and their teams. Also, they are really getting their teeth into some gnarly areas needing to be addressed. The hardest thing for me has been to step back and give them space to fail or succeed." He chuckled. "Tony tells me it's just good parenting. I told him that Fiona and I couldn't have kids. What do we know about parenting? His answer made me laugh. He said, 'looking at the kids today, what makes you think anybody understands parenting?'"

"Does that bother you?" she asked and then immediately raised her hand "Sorry. I didn't mean to get personal. ….I mean. Not having had the experience of parenting to relate to leading your team. Does that bother you?"

Moris gave a rueful smile, "No. Not really. I'm getting quite a lot out of the coaching with Tony and this is one area that feels really right to me. Maybe it might be easier if I had some actual parenting experience. I don't know. But it makes real sense. He's very good at explaining things in ways you can understand. Plus, he doesn't stretch your mind too far into psychospace with concepts that you have to work hard to grasp."

"For instance?"

Moris thought for a bit. "Well….his view that modern leadership is in a real crisis. I have to say that the more I think about it and what we talk about, the more I'm inclined to agree with him."

"What does he say?"

"There are a number of things but all combined suggest that modern leadership is way too shallow and some serious rethinking of our leadership notions needs to happen to enable a deeper, more considered and contemporary form of leadership to emerge and be cultivated.

"He believes that the term 'Leader' is itself now an issue. It is commoditised to the point that people see it as a job title or role within a hierarchy rather than attributes and characteristics that unconsciously assert themselves within a person and the make them someone others want to follow. Leadership has been reduced to a set of capabilities and practices that are 'taught'. Not learned."

"Oh. I like that," mused Maureen

"Gosh, I even googled leadership and very quickly found dozens of websites that promised to make you into a good leader in just 5 easy lessons! Or by reading this book and subscribing to our newsletter…."

"Kids are being groomed at very young ages for leadership and it is constantly being reinforced that it is a career choice. Imagine their disappointment when they find that isn't the case. On the other side of that, younger and younger people are being thrust into roles that they are underprepared for and everyone suffers the fallout from failure. It results in a lack of resilience and workforce sustainability. One that leaders are not able to deal with."

"You know. I think he's right on that account. I thought it was just my age and bias, but I do believe that senior level people aren't quite of the same…robustness, as what I've known in the past."

"Tony calls it ' the cult of fast food leadership' and describes it as, smells good, looks good and tastes good, so it is immediately gratifying. But he warns that it has very little nutrition and creates longer term workforce health issues."

Maureen frowned and asked, "So what does he think the answer is? I'm guessing he doesn't have five easy lessons or a web newsletter?"

Moris chuckled, "No. But what he is saying makes real sense if you are prepared to question and challenge what seems to be the current ideology around the subject of leadership. I know I was a bit sceptical at first but it's hard to ignore the reasoning and simple logic behind what he poses."

"I'm intrigued. Tell me a bit more about this."

"Okay. But I warn you. You may not like some of his reasoning or even agree with it. I didn't at first, and he didn't try to convince me. He just asked me to wonder, what if we are getting it wrong? He challenged me to look more closely to understand if some of today's 'accepted truisms' are actually backed up by solid evidence."

"Like what? What's one his more contentious views?" queried Maureen.

"Well, building on what I said earlier, this whole idea that you can be trained to be leader…

"It's like training a kitten to be a cat. Or a child to be an adult. When you look at it like that you see how ridiculous the notion of training to become a leader actually is. Especially, as you and I both know, leadership means many things to many people and there is often disagreement as to what it looks like. It can be very intangible. It is contextual, cultural, changeable and really comes down to being human. I remember being asked once, years ago, if I would attend a course to learn all about authentic leadership. Wouldn't that make the course an oxymoron?"

Maureen laughed, "Yes I remember that. A lot of people went along with all of that and a lot of people came back justifying their narcissism as just them being authentic. Tell me more about Tony's view on modern leadership."

"So. I'll try to describe it just as he described it to me for a start. Are you familiar with the work of Daniel Goleman and the Leadership styles?"

"Yes. I am. It's material I include in my talks with the Women in Leadership sessions at the Governance Institute."

"Tony believes there is a new, developing, level of leadership. One that is deeper than the other styles. One that is more relevant to today's world. In fact he stresses that the styles outlined by Goleman were reflective of societal styles and behavioural expectations prevalent during specific work eras of the day. Even though they are all applicable for different contexts today, the one that is emerging as the greatest need in today's world of hybrid work, slash life, is what he calls the 'Cultivating' style." Moris signalled quotation marks with his hands as he said this.

He paused as Maureen looked to be processing what he'd just said. She cocked one eyebrow at him and signalled for him to continue.

"Yes. Cultivating. I had to think hard about this. It means, to grow people. To protect them and help them to develop and thrive. A bit like the Coaching style, only, as Tony puts it, much more like a parent and mentor. It's less about work skills and capabilities, and more about building self sufficiency for wellness and resilience in the whole person.

"As I said earlier, people are getting into roles that they are often not really prepared for. Undercooked. To make things more complicated, for some time now, especially in western societies, kids are growing up protected from real opportunities to build resilience. Research suggests there there is actually a 'molly-coddled' generation happening. So in effect, we have been progressively creating a more dependent, less resilient, generation.

"Shifts in rules and regulations governing life in general has created quite a mismatch of expectations around personal responsibility and sense of entitlement. Especially when it comes to safety and wellness. So much more is put onto employers regarding a person's all round wellness that it is very difficult to know what to do. Notions of what is psychologically safe and unsafe have shifted radically over the last couple of decades. As he puts it…once you just gritted your teeth and laughed off the odd Irish joke. Now you find people taking medication to deal with PTSD from being told one.

"All of this together, along with the trends around hybrid working, technology advances, homelife pressures such as childcare with two parents working …." Moris shrugged and held his hands up. "There is a deepening and widening void in people's lives around building mental strength, dealing with disappointment and growing emotional intelligence. Modern leaders need to find ways to carefully toughen people up."

Maureen sat back and frowned. "You mean, the old 'harden up' message?"

"No. I mean…put it this way. People spend fortunes on going to the gym to put their bodies through stress and sometimes physical pain in order to improve and sustain health and fitness. Mental health and fitness is just as important, maybe more so. But we have this absolute aversion to experiencing any kind of psychological pain and we do everything we can to avoid it. Even though we know that enduring some of that pain and learning from it makes you psychologically fitter and healthier. We need to figure out how to build that 'head fitness' as Tony calls it, rather than avoiding it. Modern leaders seem to spend a lot of time protecting people from it. Perhaps we need to sit that on it's head a bit.

"The best way to become a good or a great leader is to live through experiences from which you learn. That means sometimes having bad experiences. You and I have had the benefit of that but our future leaders look to be facing quite a different world as far as that goes. So the big question is, how do we, as leaders, build our emerging leaders, and at the same time, actually lead the business?"

"So what you are saying in essence, is that we need to be less protective?" Asked Maureen.

"Essentially. But being more adept at being 'wiser heads' leaders than 'boss' leaders if you get what I mean," said Moris.

"Remember, all of the other leadership styles are still relevant. It's just this is a new challenge for leaders to face up to. Somehow we have to 'harden up' our people in a manner that recognises their sensitivities and expectations. It's best done in a caring and supportive way or they can just disengage.

"You know as an example, the other day I had to have a chat with a friend's son who is bitterly disappointed that his area of work, Data Analyst, is currently paying lower hourly rates for contractors than it did two years ago. He is angry at employers and was complaining about how unfair it is. I had to tell him that's how markets work. There has been a huge influx of workers seeking roles as there was massive layoffs in the public sector. He just couldn't get his head around that he wasn't entitled to earn more as the market shifted. In the end I had to explain that he could only really earn what others were willing to pay and if they could get the skills cheaper then why wouldn't they. I don't think he listened."

"Hmmph, I think I know what you mean. My granddaughter wrote a quite nasty review online about a store that didn't have her particular favourite colour lipgloss in stock. I was appalled at her attitude and apologised online for how she behaved. I got quite a lot of likes for that…she didn't."

" So 'Cultivating' leadership style is what Tony is calling this. I honestly believe he's right. My challenge is how to grow this in my team and live it as well when sometimes I just want to tell people to grow up. I think Leo might find this a bit of a challenge as he is a bit predisposed to a more…directive style of leadership."

"So how are we going to progress?"

"I'm planning to spend more time on personal reflection, one on one conversations and group discussions about how we focus on helping our people thrive." I'm going to insist that each of our leaders learn more about coaching, 'Volunteer ' as mentors outside of the business, and utilise personal coaches in their own development."

"Excellent," said Maureen. "Let me know if there is anything I can do to help."

"Thanks. I appreciate that. I guess patience and chats like this are two of the things I need more of."

CHAPTER 12

A SHIFT IN THINKING

As everyone wandered back into the conference room Brian muttered to Qian, " I think I'm going to enjoy this afternoon," and he grinned wickedly.

Qian glanced over toward Shona and nodded, "Me too I think," and she smiled.

"Now. Where were we?" queried Tony. "Ah yes. Culture. Talking with the exec team I am aware that this team has been charged with developing up a plan to shift the culture to be more like a High Performance Culture and to help them understand what it would like to be more strategically appropriate.

"Now I think you have a good handle on what a High Performance Culture looks like, but have you given thought to what a Strategically Appropriate Culture might look like? How we might go ahead building it here?"

Everyone looked at each other in the hope that someone might respond.

"Before we get into defining what we think the Appropriate culture is, perhaps we could digress a little and consider your views on the current context?"

Tony could sense the nervous tension in the room. No-one wanted to be first to say anything. Jerry could feel it too. Perhaps it was due to inexperience in this sort of thing? Perhaps this morning had just been too much for them.

He looked over at Tony and could see that he was prepared to wait for a response. He had a whiteboard pen poised to start gathering ideas....

Things were starting to feel a little uncomfortable and Jerry was just about to say something when Shona spoke up.

"You said something earlier about work cultures during different work eras having organisational cultures consistent with the times they were in. That work cultures pretty much reflected societal culture of the day."

"Yes I did."

"So wouldn't we want to build a culture that does just that?"

"What do others think?" asked Tony

"Sounds like a good place to start," ventured Qian

"Okay. So what are you suggesting?" Tony directed his question to Shona.

"Well. I think it's really big. Hard to really get my head around. But our society today is really diverse and we have lots of different views that affect decisions and.... should we be trying to operate more democratically? I'm struggling to understand how you run company like a society is run."

"How does everyone else feel about this?" asked Tony

"I think it's a good point," said Brian. "Is this too big for us?"

"It is a good point," said Tony. "And one which comes up quite a bit. Let me see if this'll help give it a bit more perspective and make things a little easier for us."

As he walked across the floor in front of the table he continued to speak.

"We are talking about organisational culture. It is actually a different thing from societal culture. Yes, organisation culture is influenced by the communities and societies it operates within but it is more easily defined to a degree that is useful for our purposes. One way of doing this is to spend time understanding more about your specific stakeholders and viewing them as your 'Society' rather than trying to take, or copy a national culture perspective. The type of staff you need to employ, the type of customers you are trying to attract, the expectations and interests of the shareholders, represented by your board. You'll want to think about where you do business, and perhaps some uber-trends like flexible/hybrid work. I think though that the real key to defining your Strategically Appropriate Culture lies in a real understanding of Employment Value Propositions."

Tony could feel all eyes upon him as he paced across the floor.

"Let me use an example. Military, and Churches. They exhibit strong specific cultures relative to the belief set they have but they are generally a small part of the larger society's culture that they exist in. Imagine a whole country behaving as a military body. And… You should note. Both of those types of organisations are struggling to maintain their positions and attract employees in today's world.

"In the past, these two institutions, were seen as the template for developing organisational culture. Clear sets of values and beliefs identified, promulgated and reinforced through alignment of policies, practices and people. It was relatively easy in the past to collect together, groups of people who shared strong affiliations. The military, was about having a strong force of people dedicated to physical protection and security. Churches were about faith, emotion and spirituality. Both have their own special rites and rituals, symbols, stories and hierarchies. Both presenting strong values propositions to their target audiences.

"This is exactly how business and other organisations have designed and engineered things. We've used pretty much the same tools and techniques to get everyone marching in the same direction."

He turned his eyes toward Shona

"Shona. I'm looking at you because you have the most recent academic background in this. Do you think there is anything essentially wrong in what I have said? Especially about values, beliefs and alignment?" Tony gazed at Shona until she responded.

"Well it isn't as simple as that but I guess …pretty much."

"Okay. Stay with me folks…the business world has followed the same strategy. It has worked to a degree, for some time. I believe, and the evidence is starting to emerge in support of my belief, that we need to significantly change tack. Context has changed significantly."

Tony continued to pace. Jerry noticed how this kept all eyes in the room focused. "The guy's a real pro," he thought to himself

"The tools and techniques we have used in the past are no longer relevant. Most especially in countries where there is substantial diversity within the population, high levels of freedom of speech, choice, and thought, and constitutional frameworks supportive of equality and fairness.

"Now I'm generalising here and want to avoid getting into deep and meaningful rabbit holes on this subject right now. It's more important that today, we just understand the concept rather than argue points of detail."

Tony stopped moving. He turned and looked at the team. He raised his eyebrows and then continued.

"In short then. With the diversity of people within our workforces, why do we still seem to think that aligning them and our practices, with a set of values that may have no or little attraction for them, is a good thing? I think the time has come for us to stop this archaic nonsense and get real about organisational culture as a cornerstone of success. In the past, organisation success was due to strong alignment of a set of values that were reflective of the workforce of the day. Workforces were generally more likely to be made up of people with similar backgrounds, experiences and even beliefs and interests.

"It's a hell of a lot more complex today as the workforce is much more diverse in its makeup. Not just ethnically, but all of the other demographics are in play now. Also, there is a much stronger sense of personal identity and being recognised for that in the workplace. Getting people to sing the same song with the same words, in the same language, is simply not going to work anymore. To suggest that we continue to do what we did in the past is just lazy organisational psychology. The rules have changed, so our game needs to adapt."

Tony looked over toward Jerry who was watching Shona and the others closely for their reactions. Mostly though he was interested in Shona's reaction. He wasn't disappointed. She was sitting very upright in her seat like she was ready to pounce into action and she was fairly bristling.

The others looked relaxed and attentive.

Shona stayed quiet....

"It is critical now, more than ever, that organisations put greater effort into 'inclusivity'. That means involving staff in conversations about organisation priorities/imperatives, and inviting them to consider how best to achieve those things. Instead of engaging staff in discussions about values and behaviours. They've grown up having those conversations.

"In fact. I believe it is up to the leadership to grapple with, and set the organisation's cultural parameters. They should do this by example. Not slogans.

"It is time to treat treat staff as grown up stakeholders in striving for achievement rather than as children needing good behaviour to be spelled out. Conversations about *how* to achieve can include some reference to behaviours relevant to the specific business unit having the conversation."

Tony paused and slowly scanned the faces around the room. He could see people looked thoughtful....even Shona. She was frowning down at her hands on the table top and her shoulders appeared to be in a bit of a slump.

Jerry looked over toward Tony and gave a little nod of his head.

"How does everyone feel about what I just said?" queried Tony.

"Well I..." began Shona and then took a deep breath. "I have never thought of it like this. The way you say it kinda makes sense. But what about all the research into culture? What about the experts who generally promote values and behaviours, culture assessment tools and all the training.... Surely Culture still comes down to how people behave with each other. What about...."

She tailed off, obviously looking for words.

Tony held up his hand and addressed everyone in the room.

"Shona makes some good points and I don't think we should get the idea that everything is wrong. Look. I've been around for some time in the 'culture change' world. I've done more than my fair share of implementing things that failed. Just as much as things that worked. To be honest though, it's difficult not to be cynical about something that has become an industry in itself. Over the last five or so years I've noticed a real decline in the quality of thinking being applied to building appropriate organisational cultures.

"Every second person you meet seems to be an expert in 'business transformation' or 'culture enhancement' or, and this is my pet hate….'leadership coaching'. Where did they all come from within the last decade? What have they actually done besides an online course and get a certificate? I've never met many of them in the arena, so to speak. And I've been in a lot of arenas. Even our universities aren't immune to putting forward very shallow levels of 'evidence' in support of theories or views.

"I don't want to sound too negative but I think we need people to look deeper and stop just reinforcing popular ideas. Again, it's just lazy. A paint by numbers exercise."

Brian put his hand in the air, "Can I ask, what sort of thing? An example perhaps?"

"Sure," said Tony "I'll give you a couple…

"A recent television interview with a Professor of HR at a large university talked about the question of whether hybrid working was good for productivity. It's very topical now as we all know and it has major implications for exactly what we are discussing. The item was under the headline..'Hybrid working increases productivity.'

"The Professor had recently conducted some research into hybrid working. His statement to the interviewer was "My findings were clear. Yes. Hybrid working is good for productivity. I asked x number of workers and they were adamant that it was good for their productivity. Around 75% said Yes."

Tony paused (mostly for effect). " Now can anybody tell me how this is an actual measure of productivity? No. It isn't. Yet the media accepted it as a new truth. Quite frankly, it isn't very rigorous research at all. Popular mythology is what I call it."

"Yet another is the whole GenZ, Millenial, Baby Boomer stuff…Widely accepted and promoted by consultants and, many HR people around the world, yet….there is no research at all that supports the notion that there are differences at all. In fact, research shows otherwise. For instance a major global consultancy research exercise in 2023 found that workers of all ages want the same things from their work experience.

"So why is this stuff given airtime? Why aren't scholars and professionals actually doing the work and telling the real story? If we just accept what we are told then we run the risk of actually missing the target."

At this point Jerry stood up, "Can I try and answer that question?" Tony raised his hands in a signal to go ahead.

"Well. I think that the story is sexier than the truth. People want to believe it. Given what you said about the amount of 'experts' around I would say also it has to do with money. People are more willing to pay for the promise of the sexy story and so a lot of people are profiting from promulgating these things."

"Well I agree essentially," said Tony, "But also, leaders aren't being given the space and time to really understand and, as I often say, they are undercooked anyway. They are grasping at things that sound like they will help them succeed. Ultimately we end up with a lot of emperor's new clothes situations."

"So my question of this team is what do you want to do? Follow the crowd and likely end up with more of the same mediocrity or step out from the crowd and try something more deep and meaningful?"

Everyone was looking around at everyone else. Finally, Shona broke the silence.

"Let's do it right," she said. "Let's step out from the crowd!" and with that, the team all applauded.

Tony looked over to Jerry and grinned broadly. "Over to you now," he said.

Jerry laughed and went over the whiteboard.

"Thanks everyone," he said. "Now as you know we have been working with a new concept known as Triple Knot thinking. Tony mentioned that one of the things we should get our heads around that would greatly help define the Appropriate Culture was Employment Value Propositions.

I'd like to introduce you all to the Employment Value Triple Knot."

He began to draw....

CHAPTER 13

INVESTIGATION

It was the day of mediation with Averil and her lawyer. Moris had decided not to attend on the advice of the company legal counsel. Jerry would go along with full authority to make decisions if needed.

Even though Moris knew that the allegations against him were completely false, he felt nervous. Often, these types of things could go awry due to difficulties in disproving the lies and, as Wiremu put it, a bias of sympathy for the poor defenceless victim versus the corporate monster. If things couldn't be settled at mediation then they may get nasty and, despite the untruth of it, reputations could be irrevocably damaged.

It rankled. Especially as Moris had been nothing but supportive of Averil during her time at the company. He just couldn't understand why she was doing this.

He was keeping his cellphone handy so he could get promised updates and developments. Wiremu had advised him that today would likely mostly revolve around trying to understand Averil's position. To date there had been no evidence provided in support of her accusations of bullying. He would contact Moris during a break to let him know what new information had come up.

Moris settled back into his chair and sighed deeply. Well, he thought, I guess things could be a lot worse. Everyday he could sense that morale was lifting and things around the office felt a lot more positive. He frowned, all except for the nagging feeling that he'd somehow done something to offend both Gordon and Susan. They were both quite curt and standoffish with him over the last few weeks. He promised himself that he'd talk to each of them before the end of the week.

Right now he wanted to just note down the key points from his coaching conversation with Tony this morning. They were good points and worth discussing with his leadership team as part of their development. He took out his journal and began to write. He made a list of the points:

Leadership isn't a role in a hierarchy. It's more a set of attributes and characteristics that a person applies dependent on context and the situation. Probably the biggest thing is to be able to read the situation and act appropriately. Leaders unconsciously adapt their style to fit the context.

There is a new style emerging as the context of organisational life has shifted dramatically. The new style is 'Cultivating'. The leader who grows others and builds resilience.

Good leaders are able to easily relate to the area of work they are in. Quickly gaining a deep understanding of the area you are leading is crucial to credibility. In fact, many of the very best leaders come from within. They've been in the arena and those they lead respect that..

You don't train people to become leaders. You cultivate leaders through nurturing them through experiences and if they show real leadership potential hone it. Some training can be useful but only after a person has adopted an authentic leadership mindset. Remember, experience is the best way to learn. You don't learn leadership at a course or from a book.

Not everyone can be a leader. It's a nonsense to think that and some people who push themselves forward as aspiring leaders are exactly those you don't want. Watch for this.

Leadership has nothing to do with gender and /or diversity so resist the pressure to promote based on anything other than merit. But make sure merit is defined correctly.

It didn't look like a long list. Especially given that they had been talking for at least an hour. Still, it certainly was a thought provoking list and for Moris, most especially point number (2). He had much to reflect on regarding the implications for this business.

The last one would be tricky to address. Especially given the Board Chair's interest in growing women in leadership.

He was pondering this when the phone rang.

"Yes?" Moris held the handset to his ear.

"Hi Moris, it's Jerry here. Have you got time for a chat on this? I can put you on speaker here so Wiremu can join in."

"Yes. I've left my diary open this morning to make sure I was available for this. Go ahead."

"Okay. We've just finished listening to Averil's counsel rage against the organisation for allowing bullying to go on. I have to say a lot of noise and bluster. But essentially, no evidence was presented to support this other than Averil saying it was true. We did ask for specifics and didn't get any. Just more claims of 'multiple occasions of you shouting at her and telling her to do things or else.'"

"Or else what?" asked Moris

"Good question. We asked it as well and didn't get any answer."

"So now it's our turn to respond and we are just breaking for 10 minutes while we consider what they have said. Oh, and by the way they have suggested a settlement of $50k for hurt and humiliation and three months salary in lieu of notice for being forced to resign."

"What?" exclaimed Moris. "Are you kidding?"

"Moris. It's Wiremu here. This isn't unusual from this lawyer. Don't fret. As I see it there is no evidence to support these claims and at this stage no reason to even consider agreeing a settlement."

"So what do you think we do?"

"My advice is to say exactly that and tell them that we don't agree that there has been any bullying whatsoever. Then we can see if they suddenly produce anything of merit in their claims. If not then I actually think we call their bluff and tell them we do not agree that there is anything to be resolved. In the meantime we reiterate our demand for Averil to stop making defaming statements or we will need to pursue legal action. I know it is a tough standpoint but they really don't seem to have anything of substance to this."

Moris thought for a while. He didn't like conflict and was generally averse to threatening strong legal action but hell! He had done nothing wrong. Guess it is time for some situational leadership," he thought ruefully.

"Okay then. Please go ahead. You're the experts."

~

Susan looked around the records room in despair. There were boxes and boxes of files and various paperwork piled up in every corner of the room. As well as that, there were filing cabinets chock full of stuff. How on earth was she going to find what she was hoping for in here?

She and Gordon had agreed that they really needed more hard evidence of wrongdoing before they talked to anybody else. "I mean. The CEO looks to have been siphoning out regular sums of money into a private account," she thought. Serious stuff.

Susan took a deep breath and blew out her cheeks. "Well. Can't stand here staring. Gotta get into it." She decided to start with the boxes marked finance and tried to locate those within a date range of the last 5 to 6 months. Actually, that wasn't so hard. The boxes were all well labeled. Each box was about the size of a carton of 12 bottles of wine. Susan smiled to herself. "How did she think of that for a description?"

Anyway, she started digging into each box and soon found that Leila, the Finance assistant, had been quite diligent in ensuring each invoice was attached to relevant receipts and where there may have been a receipt missing, a note was made of the reason why. Generally, these were really small amounts and were for things like coffees etc. She must remember to commend Leila for a job well done after all of this was sorted.

She wasn't really sure what she expected to see but she stuck to the task and before long she had three boxes stacked up beside her. Only about 50 more to go she thought ruefully. After what seemed like about an hour her eyes started to tire and she thought to herself that perhaps it would be good time for a break. She was just getting up from amidst the pile of boxes and papers around her when the door opened.

"Susan!" exclaimed Gordon as he stepped around the mess on the floor. "I've been looking for you all over the place. What on earth are you doing in here at this time of the evening?"

"What time is it?" asked Susan with a frown.

"It's six thirty. We're supposed to be going out to the theatre tonight. I was worried when I couldn't get hold of you on your phone and so went to your office. The phone was on the desk. Lucky I saw the light under this door as I was heading out to the carpark. What are you doing?"

Susan looked at Gordon. Her eyes widening,

Six thirty. Damn. "Will I have time to get home and changed? I didn't realise it was so late. I'll lock this door and take the key that's normally sitting with reception."

"C'mon," said Gordon "I'll drive you home and you can put your face on in the car as we go. Although you don't really need to put makeup on as you have a very pretty…"

"Gordon. Stop it," she giggled shyly. "Let's go. Can't be late for the show."

As they were getting into the car Gordon asked, "So I'm assuming that you were looking for leads in the records room?"asked Gordon.

"Yes, " she sighed. "But I didn't find anything. I'll have to go in and tidy it all up in the morning."

"No problem," said Gordon "Why don't I come in early as well and together we can see if there is anything of use in there." He chuckled, "We'll have to be careful to leave before others come into the office or they might find us both there and think that something is going on between us."

"You mean there *isn't* anything going on between us?" asked Susan teasingly.

"Well, I…" stuttered Gordon

"At least not until after the show," continued Susan putting her hand over his on the steering wheel.

"Ahh, w..what do you mean?" said Gordon nervously.

"Well. My car is still at the office and I will need a knight in shining armour to take me home tonight," she breathed.

Gordon gulped and nodded his head. "Okay," he managed to say.

~

The next morning Gordon and Susan arrived quite early at the office. Needless to say that they were both in a very happy mood and Gordon was even humming a tune.

The records room looked worse than Susan remembered but that could have been her tiredness.

"What were you trying to find?" asked Gordon.

"I don't really know. I was just hoping to see something that might look like it was out of place."

"Okay. Can I suggest something then?" he asked.

"Of course," said Susan "Just as long as you keep it seemly…" and she arched her eyebrow at him. Gordon flushed and looked down at his feet.

"I was just thinking. As Engineers do. Logically. Why not firstly just find the receipts and invoices that have been signed by Moris as a starting point? As you know. We all have authority to sign but none of us could sign up to the level of the CEO."

"Okay. Good idea. It's way more methodical than I've been doing. If you take those boxes over there I'll sift through these ones and pull out all of the ones with Moris' signature on them. Unless of course somebody else is to blame, and in that case we could at least eliminate Moris."

They had about an hour before staff were due into the office and so they decided to tidy up the mess first and just transfer any Moris signed docs into an empty file box so they could look at them later. They would need to work fast however.

Pretty soon they had filled two file boxes of signed invoices and receipts and Gordon suggested that they stop there for now and take a closer look later. Susan agreed. These documents were from the 3 months immediately after the last CEO had 'resigned' so, she thought, most likely to be ones that would show anything as that would have been the most opportune time for things to pass with less scrutiny.

They quickly took the boxes out to Gordon's car and popped them into the boot. "We can have a look at them after work at my place if you like?" suggested Gordon "I have more room there and we can spread out the papers more easily. If you don't mind having takeaway food then we can really motor."

"Sounds like a plan,"said Susan and turned to go. She hesitated and then urned toward Gordon. "I'm worried about this you know."

"I know. What if we find that Moris has been doing wrong? I'm worried too."

"I almost hope we don't find anything. I've come to quite like Moris and I'm especially excited at how things are developing with the Triple Knot stuff. It'd be a real shame to lose that. I really think it has fantastic possibilities."

"You know Susan. I have been thinking exactly the same." Gordon frowned.

~

Wiremu, and Jerry were with Moris in his office.

"No result. I thought that would be the case. Now it's really over to them to take the next step," advised Wiremu.

"Which is?" queried Moris

Wiremu looked over to Jerry who answered.

"Well. They either file a grievance with the Employment court, in which case we will then see what the evidence is around bullying. Or, they might make another offer to settle. I think we would be confident that they don't have any smoking gun if they come back with an offer.

Having said all that, it's never really a good thing to end up in court over these things. Mud sticks, and the cost of this could be high. It wouldn't be unusual for a judge to award costs to the employee. They often seem to lean toward the worker and not the employer. We may have to consider a legal course of action around defamation. Gotta say though, that can get quite dirty,"

Wiremu was nodding at this and he added, "I'd rather not go down that road but if she continues to badmouth the company on social media then we may have no option but to push. I have already sent her a cease and desist letter and we haven't seen any new things being posted for a while."

"I'm more worried about the mud sticking and the impact internally on staff. Averil has a lot of friends here. Plus, I think we are just starting to come to grips with the Triple Knot and new leadership thinking and this sort of thing could derail a lot of good work." Moris sounded frustrated. "I only wish I could understand why the hell she is doing this."

Jerry sighed loudly,"Me too. I guess we'll just have to wait and see what their next move is."

CHAPTER 14

FINDING THE ISSUE

The Workplace Triple Knot idea was giving both Gordon and Leo a few headaches. It was not as simple as they'd first thought, once they started to dig into it more.

They both agreed that the idea behind the three environments was logical. But it wasn't clear how you could use that to do something on a practical basis that would positively impact the company. They really did need an HR person to help. They talked to Jerry and he'd given it some thought.

He was sitting in the board room with them now, ready to share his thoughts.

"To be honest, I think this is the most interesting Triple Knot there is," he said.

"I'd love to be spending more time on this but I'm swamped. I do see there is a real need for some strategic HR and Organisation Development thinking to be part of this. So I think that this is a great opportunity to have someone else from my team involved. They will be able to concentrate on this and I can make sure other work they have gets reprioritised."

Leo looked over at Jerry. " Do we really want to be floating this stuff below the exec level? I mean, just yet? Shouldn't we at least we should do some more 'direction setting' stuff before we open the game up for staff. Don't you think?'

"Actually. No. I don't think so." Jerry poured himself a glass of water from the carafe on the table. Leo and Gordon shared a glance and waited.

"I think it's well past time that we got more of our people involved. Especially staff who have knowledge and skills that can contribute to the work we need to do. We don't know everything and we can't do everything. Just because we are more senior doesn't endow us with better ideas than others. Also, the earlier we bring people into this, the more chance we have of it succeeding. It builds trust and ownership. Those are two really key things when you are driving change of any kind."

Leo rubbed his chin thoughtfully. Gordon tilted his head and looked directly at Jerry. "So what's your thinking then? Who do see from your team working with us on this?"

Jerry looked at at Leo and then back to Gordon. He took a short breath "Shona."

"Really?" exclaimed Leo. "I thought she was ....an issue?"

"Yep," said Jerry. "She can be. But I know she has the skills and knowledge needed for this work. Her job is Organisation Development and that's exactly what the core of this Triple Knot is. It's about how the bits all work together to enhance how employees work together and improve organisational performance."

"Well. She hasn't been doing a great job of it so far has she? We haven't been doing all that well have we?" quipped Leo.

"C'mon Leo. We can't blame her for that. If anything, we, the SLT, carry more blame than anyone. Remember, ultimately it's us who set the set the gameplan for the players to perform. I think you'd agree that we haven't really spent a lot of time on that. Now we are. And remember, we are shifting toward a more contemporary style of leadership. A cultivating leader should really be giving the team opportunities to experience and learn." Jerry grinned as he said this.

"And fail," said Leo.

"Yes. That too. Best lessons I ever had were my failures."

"Gordon. You haven't said much. What do you think?"

Gordon had been sitting with his arms folded across his chest. Now he leaned forward and placed his elbows on the table. He put his hands together as if he was praying and placed his fingertips under his chin. "I say…why not? If she she can help us then we'd be stupid not to involve her. And for all of the other reasons you just gave." He sighed. " Although I do have one concern."

Jerry raised his eyebrows in a signal to continue.

"She always comes across as a real know-it all. Plus she tells you how you have to do this and that and a whole range of woolly things."

Jerry laughed.

"Yes. I think you'll find that she may have changed a bit. We had a really good chat recently after a full day session with the whole HR team. Tony was at that session as well. Afterward, she opened up to me that she was never really comfortable with a lot of the 'accepted' views on driving organisation change and in particular, making a real high performing organisation. She admitted that she probably came across as a process follower rather than as a creator and generator of solutions. It was a really good, deep and meaningful conversation. I told her that I understood. People often come through university thinking that what they have been taught there is the right way to do things. I pointed out to her that she needed to focus on the outcomes and principles and not stay locked into what others have done to achieve them. I think she gets it now.

Still. If it becomes an issue working with her. Tell me."

Gordon looked over to Leo and after a pause Leo nodded.

"OK looks like we have a new team member," announced Gordon.

∼

Later that afternoon Gordon found his feet taking him out to the carpark in a rush. He'd ordered Indian takeaways and he needed to get home before they were delivered. Susan was going to meet him there having gone home a little earlier to sort out some things for her nephew.

As he climbed into his car he thought to himself. "What do we do next? If we do find something wrong that is." He chewed over this question as he drove the few kilometres to his home.

He got there just as the delivery guy arrived with his food. There, parked across the road, he saw Susan getting out of her car. She looked tense as well.

"Let's eat first and then we can get into these files," suggested Gordon. Susan nodded and they went into the lounge. The dining room was full of boxes which Gordon had dropped off during his lunch hour and there was no room to sit and have dinner at the table.

After about fifteen minutes, they both laughed as Susan said it felt like they were teenagers eating out of boxes in front of the telly.

As they ate, Gordon looked at Susan and said, "I've been pondering about what to do if we find something bad. I think we might need to have a quiet word with Jerry to make sure we do things the right way, I know this is kind of his gig."

"I hate to say this but, do you trust him?" asked Susan in a quiet voice.

Gordon looked over his left shoulder toward the pile of boxes on the kitchen table and paused before answering. "Yes. I do. Besides. I don't really think we have too many options do we?"

Susan pushed a lock of hair away from her eyes as she looked at him. She bit her lip and nodded. "Okay."

"Well. Let's get started," said Gordon, finishing up his meal.

They both took a box each. Pretty soon there was paper strewn all over the floor.

Susan looked exasperated as she said, " This is hopeless. I don't even know what we're looking for!"

"Hmmm." Gordon was staring at two different documents, one in his left hand and the other in his right.

"I don't really know if this is anything but look at this." He held out the copies to Susan.

"What am I looking at?" she asked.

"Well. Most of these documents have been initialled by Moris but every now and again I find one that has his whole signature on it. Is that unusual? I've just noticed it and perhaps it is because some are for bigger amounts?"

"Hang on a minute," frowned Susan. "Can we separate the full signatures out from the initialled ones? Just to see if you're right and there is a pattern. Although our policy doesn't say anything like that from memory."

In about twenty minutes there were two neat piles in front of them. The one on the left had been initialled and was quite a large pile. The other had full signatures and was much smaller. Only about a dozen in total.

"Do you see a pattern? I sure as hell can't," said Susan.

"No…me eith….wait…Holy shit!" exhaled Gordon

"What.? What is it?" asked Susan, feeling the tension in the air.

"It's these documents with Moris' full signature on them." Gordon looked up at Susan. He had a stupid grin on his face. "Look," he said as he held one out.

"I can't see anything," said Susan, quite flustered now.

"It's the signature. It's wrong."

"What do you mean? What's wrong with it?"

"Well. Who do you know that would write their own name wrong?"

Susan looked again. "I can't see what you mean. That's Moris' name"

"Well no it's not actually. Moris always signs his last name with a little tail under the letter 'a' . It's a thing called an ogonek. I know because I asked him about it once and he explained that it's often used in Polish vowels. Look. There isn't one on these signatures but I know he uses it. He told me that he feels it important that when he signs things with his full signature then he always makes it official. I've seen him do it."

Susan's mouth dropped open. "Oh my god. Wait! Let me just get into my laptop. I have an e copy of my employment contract. I'm pretty sure Moris put his whole signature on that."

As Susan connected her laptop up and accessed the files Gordon continued to scrutinise the documents.

"I have it!" exclaimed Susan excitedly. "Yes. Here is his complete signature." She held the laptop up so Gordon could look at it.

Gordon pushed his right cheek out with his tongue. "Wow. It's clearly showing the ogonek."

They looked at each other. "It's forged!" they blurted out together and then laughed.

"And I think I know who forged it," said Gordon.

"What do we do now?" asked Susan wide eyed, once Gordon had told her about his suspicion.

"I think we still need to talk to Jerry. But I think we should include Moris in that conversation."

"In the morning. Right?" asked Susan.

Gordon had wicked gleam in his eye. "Of course in the morning. I have something more important to do tonight," he said as he looked at Susan.

"Yeess…?" Susan said quietly.

"Well. There's a bloody mess of papers and boxes all over my kitchen. I need to clean it up!" he announced.

"You bastard.." Susan laughed, as she threw an empty cardboard food carton at him.

CHAPTER 15

DISCLOSING THE SECRET

T he following morning started bright and sunny. It was like a sign that today was going to be good day. Moris was in his office early, trying to pull together the format for the upcoming Board meeting presentations. It was going to be a very busy and full agenda. The Board had set aside the whole of an afternoon to concentrate on the presentations from the management team. Maureen said they were excited and really looking forward to some innovative thinking. Moris just hoped he and the team wouldn't disappoint. From what he'd seen so far though, he was pretty buoyant that they'd come up with some really great stuff.

Jerry and Wiremu were going to catch up with him this morning so they could develop a strategy around this issue with Averil and hopefully try and minimise any damage. This thing had been burning a big knot in his gut since it all started. He hated it when games were being played by people and his natural anxiety about doing things wrong kept eating at him.

There was a light knock on the door and Jerry poked his head in. "Got time for a chat?" He asked.

"Well, actually. We are meeting in about half an hour and I have quite a bit to do. Is it something that can wait?"

"I think you'll want to know about this before Wiremu drops by," Jerry suggested.

Moris groaned and sat back in his chair. He waved Jerry in "Okay. Let's have it," he said resignedly. So much for the good day!

Jerry came in with Gordon and Susan in tow. Moris hadn't expected that.

"I think we'll need to shut the door for this." added Jerry as he shut the door.

Moris looked around at each of them. "Jerry…?" he asked.

Jerry motioned for Gordon and Susan to start.

Gordon and Susan looked at each other. Susan shrugged and nodded that he should go first.

"Well. Over the last few weeks Susan and I have been trying to figure out a problem around what looked like some ….issues in our company finances."

"How do you mean….issues?" Moris was frowning, looking directly at Susan.

"Umm," began Susan. "I noticed some fairly big spikes in our travel, advertising and design costs over the last few months. I just couldn't get things to reconcile and so I started to look. I found some larger than normal payments had been made to some of our regular suppliers but when I quizzed a couple of them they didn't know anything about it. I got especially nervous when I found that the bank account details were different from what we usually paid into."

Moris frowned deeply and leaned forward. "So how long have you been looking into this? Why didn't you let me know before? Are our reports to Board wrong?"

Susan looked down at her hands in her lap. "I've been trying to understand this for around four months now. I didn't say anything to you before …well…before I had some idea as to who might be behind it. I thought…"

Moris held up a hand and interrupted her. "You thought I was involved," he stated. Almost in a whisper. "How could you think this!" his voice was rising and everyone could see he was beginning to get angry.

"Woah. Slow down Moris." interjected Jerry. "Susan was brand new here remember. She didn't know you from a bar of soap. I think you should hear what she has to say before you react."

Moris took a deep breath. "Fair enough," he said. "But I'm not real happy that you didn't talk to me as soon as you noticed something. Why did you think I might be involved?"

Susan sat up straighter in her chair as Gordon got up and stood behind her. His hands on her shoulders.

"Well, Jerry's right. I didn't know you much at all at first. But you were the previous head of finance and I needed to know why you hadn't seen this before. It took me a while to dig back and find that it only started from the time you were made CEO. I didn't really know what to do or who to talk to but Gordon noticed I wasn't happy and offered to help."

Moris glared up at Gordon who pressed his lips together and nodded. "We needed to get some more facts before deciding what action to take. I thought it the sensible thing to do. I'm sorry we didn't talk to you first but, shit Moris. How else could we play this? I do know you. And trust you by the way. I said to Susan that we should try and find more evidence of what was really happening as we shouldn't just lay yet another issue at your feet. We really needed to be able to give you more than just our knowledge at the time. We've been digging through our files and we think we have found something really important."

The room went silent for a while. Moris looked over at Jerry who raised his hands and shrugged. He knew as much about this as Moris.

"Okay then. I'm sorry I got a bit angry. You were right to pull me back. Not a great example of Cultivating style eh? I guess I have much to learn also. So tell me. What did you find?"

"Susan? I think you should tell it," suggested Gordon.

"Well. We have found several invoices that have been signed off in your name with your signature, for money to go into bank accounts that don't belong to the businesses named on the invoice. I've contacted some of them and they don't know anything about it."

Moris was wide eyed at this. "This can't be right. I am very careful about what I sign and I know most of the businesses we use as providers. Hell, I set a lot of the relationships up!"

Susan held up her hand. "We've dug into this more and I've talked to three banks so far who have these accounts. They wouldn't tell me whose name the accounts were in but one was able to unofficially advise me that they didn't have that account number associated with that business.

"At first I was really torn but in the end Gordon sussed things out. Look at the signature on this invoice." She held out an invoice for Moris to look at. "And this ,....and this." Several more invoices were thrust forward. Jerry came around to Moris side of the desk to look at them as well.

"Can you see?"

Jerry looked totally confused.

Before anyone else could say anything Susan charged on. "As Gordon saw it first. There is no *ogonek* on these signatures. I checked this against your real signature that we have on file and clearly this is a forgery."

Moris' mouth dropped open. "But...who?"

"Gordon says he thinks he knows who."

Both Jerry and Moris looked directly at Gordon. "Averil."

There was a stunned silence.

"I checked some of her docs that I had on file and I'm no expert but I am willing to bet an expert would agree that this is her handwriting." Moris and Jerry looked at the documents closely and then stared at each other for a few moments.

Finally the silence was broken by a low whistle as Moris pursed his lips together.

"Holy shit!" he whispered. He flicked a glance to Susan and raised his eyebrows. "How much?" he asked.

"As far as I can tell at this point ..around $170 grand." She looked around at all the faces.

Moris was clearly angry. Gordon passed a reassuring look to Susan.

Jerry. Well, Jerry was positively beaming.

"What?" thought Susan "Is he happy about this?"

Finally, Jerry cleared his throat.

"Susan. I'm really sorry that you had this to stress over. It couldn't have been easy for you. Coming into a new job and having to navigate this. A darn good job that Gordon was able to help."

"Can you perhaps leave this with Moris and I from here?" he started to usher Susan and Gordon from the room but Moris spoke up.

"Susan," Moris was shaking. Obviously trying to keep his emotions in control. "Thank you." With that he put his head in his hands and started reading again.

"So what's your thought?" he asked Jerry without looking up.

"Most certainly this'll make the 'Personal Grievance' disappear if we can prove it was Averil. I think we ask Wiremu when he's here shortly."

"Yeah, but I should have been on top of this. I'll need to tell Maureen immediately. Damn, I thought we were going OK with the board but this will rock their confidence." He sighed and looked up toward the ceiling. "Timing is shit with the big session on us already."

Jerry stared straight into Moris' eye and said."Look. The whole reason this happened was because the Board had you filling in for a while doing 2 jobs. Then it was a new person whom you had to hand the keys of finance to. With all of this going on I think it'd be a pretty poor Board who feel aggrieved with you. Remember, it was somebody who was clever enough to do this when things were all a bit in the air. No way anybody in your position could have been over all of this. Talk to Maureen and see what she says. I'm happy to give her my views if you want as well."

They were interrupted by a knock at the door. "That'll be Wiremu. Let's get his view before you talk to Maureen eh?" Moris nodded and waved a hand toward the door. "OK. Let him in."

Jerry crossed to the door and opened it for Wiremu to enter.

"Hi guys. Ready to brainstorm?"

There was no response and Wiremu became aware of an atmosphere in the room.

"What's happened?" he asked.

Jerry was smiling but Moris was fairly glowering.

"Shall I tell it?" Jerry asked Moris, who nodded. As Jerry talked, Wiremu's eyes grew wide.

At last Jerry completed the story. There was a stony silence. Wiremu looked over to Moris and asked, "Why are you so glum? If it can be proved that Averil has committed fraud then we can say goodbye to the PG. In fact, you could bring an action against her. Are you considering this and going to the Police?"

Moris thought for a couple of seconds and responded. "To be perfectly honest I'm not yet sure of what to do. First I have to let the Board Chair know and I need to do that this morning. Can I do that first and then we can have another chat? I'm really sorry but can I ask both of you to perhaps go and grab a coffee or something while I call Maureen?"

"Well. OK. But you know my view on this," said Jerry

Wiremu inclined his head to the left and said. "If Maureen wants any legal view please tell her I would be happy to help."

Jerry promised to be back within a half hour and said he'd bring Moris a decent strong black coffee. Moris picked up his mobile as Jerry and Wiremu shut the door behind them.

Maureen answered the phone almost immediately. "Hi Moris what's up?"

Moris took a deep breath and began to tell Maureen of this morning's development.

~

As Wiremu walked to the cafe alongside Jerry he asked, "So. Your thoughts?"

"I say we go hard at this. Averil and her warrior were fairly unforgiving in their attacks on Moris and I believe we need to respond in kind."

"How can you be certain this was Averil though?"

"We can't. Not yet anyway. But I have a contact. A private investigator who is very adept at this kind of thing. I think we should ask him to concentrate on finding out who owns the bank account where the money has been going to, and also get a handwriting expert to verify the signatures and whose hand penned them."

"Okay. But we'd need to move quickly. What I didn't get a chance to tell you yet is that we received notice this morning from Averil's counsel that they would be filing in the Employment Relations Authority in two days unless we are able to provide a suitable settlement offer.

"It would be much better if we could take action against her before they did that, otherwise we run the risk that we would need to resolve the employment problem before the criminal one. That could get messy. Much cleaner if we could move really quickly and engage the Police with a set of compelling evidence. They may take a little while to get the wheels of justice turning but at least we could show that this was underway before legal action in the employment court was initiated. I'm pretty confident that the ERA would want to wait until the Police determined whether they would prosecute or not. I know it's not completely kosher but we could argue that the employment action is a smokescreen to hide the criminal offending and it is our view that it should be resolved first rather than potentially waste the court's time. I know they are flat out and I think they'll act prudently in this."

As they walked into the cafe Jerry gave a little wave to a couple sitting at table in the corner. He then pulled out his mobile and started to search through his contacts. "I'll have a Mocha thanks," he said to Wiremu who laughed. "Oh, and an Americano for Moris please. A large one. With sugar."

By the time they returned to Moris Office, he had finished his conversation with Maureen and was sitting with his back to an open door, hands on his head and staring out of the window. He actually looked very relaxed.

Jerry stuck his head in "Coffee?" he said. Moris didn't turn around but waved him in.

Wiremu and Jerry both entered and sat down on the large sofa across from Moris' desk.

They waited.

Moris slowly turned around to face them in his swivel chair. He was positively beaming. His smile was so wide....

Jerry looked at Wiremu. They were both clearly puzzled.

"Thanks for the coffee," said Moris as he sat back in his chair and took a sip.

"Alright. I have to ask. What happened with Maureen?" queried Jerry.

"Well. Very interesting conversation. As soon as I said what our suspicions were Maureen confessed that the Board actually were aware that she may have done something wrong at a previous employer. Something, apparently, of a similar nature. In fact…" Moris leaned forward and placed his elbows on his desk. "It was my predecessor, Karen, who had convinced the Board that she was the right person for the Marketing role and that she had paid for her indiscretion. Told them that they should show trust as a good employer and give her another chance.

"Maureen said the Board were split at the time but it was a difficult recruitment environment and she was, in the end, the only candidate. Actually, Maureen apologised for not advising me of this at the time, instead, acquiescing to Karen's desire to keep it under wraps from the rest of us."

"Sooo...?" prompted Jerry. Feeling a bit miffed that he hadn't known this as the head of HR.

"So there is no problem with the Board and we should get on and do what we think is right. They will support us." Moris was smiling again.

Jerry looked over at Wiremu.

"Hi guys. Ready to brainstorm?" he grinned.

~

As soon as they left Moris office, Gordon took hold of Susan't elbow and steered her toward the outside door. "C'mon. I think we deserve a coffee."

Susan nodded and together they headed off to the cafe.

Pretty soon they were both sipping their favourite hot treat and ruminating on the morning's events.

"You did bloody well," said Gordon looking over the rim of his cup. "There's no easy way to tell a story like that."

Susan put her cup down. Shaking a little. "I was so worried. Still am a bit," she admitted. "When I saw the hurt in Moris face it was all I could do not to burst into tears. He's worked really hard. I know. I just hope he forgives us for not telling him straight away."

She dropped her head and looked so sad that Gordon was almost overcome with the desire to take her in his arms and comfort her. Instead, he said nothing and just waited.

Susan gave a sigh and picked up her cup. "Well. It's done now. We will just have to wait and see what happens next." She looked over toward the counter as Jerry and a younger man dressed in a sharp pinstripe suit came in together. "That must be Wiremu," she thought.

Jerry glanced over toward her and gave her a little wave and a thumbs up. He then took out his phone and started to make a call.

"That must be our lawyer," Susan said to Gordon. He glanced over and chuckled. "The big guy wearing the power suit? Either that or he's a hit man. Yes, that's Wiremu. I'll introduce you before they leave the cafe."

CHAPTER 16

THE PRESENTATIONS BEGIN

"Is everything ready?" Moris asked his team.

He'd walked the 5km from home to the office early this morning. It was a beautiful clear morning and probably would be quite warm in the afternoon. Still, it was a little nippy when he left so he'd put on a light wind jacket and walking shoes and set off early.

He was both excited and nervous as today was the big day. He felt refreshed and eager to start.

Now the team were all gathered in the Board room whilst the Board were in the much larger Training Suite awaiting the afternoon's session. The Board had already enjoyed a light lunch and it was now nearly 12:30pm. Time to join them.

Moris and Maureen had decided that the Training Suite was more appropriate as it had great audio visual equipment, was a much larger room and able to fit everyone comfortably. Also, as Moris pointed out, it held a more conducive atmosphere for the material that was going to be showcased, to the Board. This was an important exercise and Moris knew that they would need to pull out all of the stops and make it a day of maximum impact.

His palms were a little sweaty and he became aware that he was fidgeting with his pen a lot. He knew that the team were nervous. He trusted them to deliver but he needed to appear calm and confident in order to support them. Over the last couple of months, they'd worked damn hard to develop up this stuff.

"OK. Remember. You've done the work. Let's go and present our thoughts and treat it like a conversation. I have total confidence in you all and from what I have seen in each of the topics, I have no doubt that the Board will get it and support us in it. Let's go."

The members of the Board were all seated and looked eager as the leadership team entered the auditorium. Moris noticed the slightly surprised looks on the faces of the Board as several other staff also entered the room and took seats.

When everyone had their seats Moris addressed them. "Good afternoon everyone. It's great to see you all here. I note that some of you may be a little surprised that we have invited several other members of the overall team to attend as well. That was my doing. The ideas and initiatives that you are about to see have been pulled together by more than just the leadership team. I thought it appropriate, and critical, that all of the staff involved in building what I believe to be a very good blueprint for success, are here to see all of the component parts put together and to hear any of the discussions that we might have regarding it. We all own this. We all have a major part in making it real, and we all want it to succeed."

He looked about the room, slowly. Meeting as many eyes as possible as he scanned across the rows of seats. "Today the team are going to introduce you to a set of ideas and initiatives which, for some of you, may seem quite different. You may be skeptical, or excited, or just nervous. I can assure you though that everything you see and hear today has been subject to significant degrees of critical analysis, discussion, challenge, investigation, contemplation and refinement, before being put to you. We will cover the highlights via presentation slides but there is a more detailed document available which we will send out later today.

"Firstly though, it is important to remind ourselves of why we are here. Well, quite simply, we have been limping along on a path that, unless something major changed, would inevitably lead us to the likely demise of the company. All of the signs have been poor for a while now and you, the Board, have charged us with building a plan to reinvigorate this organisation and, in your words, '*build an enduring, healthy and thriving organisation.*'

"This of course, begs the question, 'What does an enduring, healthy and thriving organisation look like?' We believe we cannot only answer that. We can achieve it.

"This central idea has led us to question pretty much everything about our operating model and organisational system. Over time, our system has become very complex and confusing. There are many moving parts, conflicting priorities, archaic and ineffective practices and sometimes even misguided beliefs all contributing to the overall mix. Attempts over the years to improve, or change all or some of the component parts, have had mixed success but have often resulted in the introduction of even more complexity.

"The leadership team have taken this opportunity to step outside of the norm and avoid the usual diet of over engineered business improvement solutions on offer from the major consultancies, academic institutions and, media driven, flavour of the month snake-oil salesmen.

"We have instead, adopted a DIY approach to resetting our operating system. Our aim is to develop an overall system that is: Simple, sensible, and sustainable

"You will note our 'core design concept' featuring in today's presentations. We have used this concept to help us simplify and focus our efforts toward achievement of our central idea.

"This core design concept was originated and developed by Tony Delahunt. Tony is an experienced and credible senior executive and consultant. We have been lucky enough to be able to get Tony to help us to understand and utilise this core concept in crystallising our plans. I'd like to thank Tony for his guidance.

"The board have met Tony and he has spent some time with you explaining his Triple Knot concept. I am sure that you will remember this. However, please feel free to ask questions or provide comments as we move forward today.

"There will be four separate but related presentations. Each presentation will describe an organisation level Triple Knot and you will see the emergence of an organisational operating model as we start to link and combine them. We won't be diving into nth degree detail, but there will be enough for you to get a really good idea of some the things we need to do.

"Now I'm going to do less talking and hand you over to the first of the Triple Knot design teams. Jerry?" Moris looked over to Jerry who moved out of his chair and came forward.

"Hello everyone, and welcome," Jerry started off.

"As Moris indicated, we have four separate short presentations today that I hope you will both enjoy and value. Before I start I would like to thank and acknowledge the team who put a lot of time and effort into this first Triple Knot presentation. I'm not going to start a trend and name everybody as that'll likely end up today feeling like you've just sat through a whole lot of Academy Award speeches.

"Can I please just ask the team to all stand up?" Everyone who worked on the first Triple Knot stood up and let the Board see who they were.

"I want to introduce you to the first of the Triple Knots that you will see today: This is the Organisational Sustainability Triple Knot."

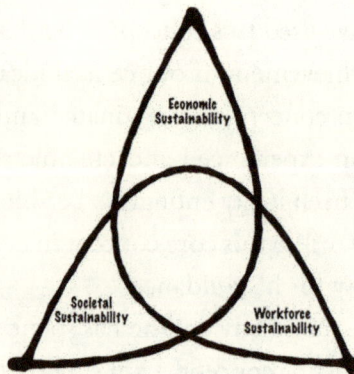

A diagram appeared on the screen behind Jerry.

"The relationship between these three elements is critical to the ongoing health of any organisation. In the past, sustainability has been looked at through an environmental lens and conversations usually revolve around green policies and carbon footprints.

"Those are important but actually, what we are looking at, is a model that makes us ask ourselves questions around how financial decisions maintain ongoing business viability. How we grow and refresh our people capabilities to stay relevant in the labour markets, retain, transfer and manage knowledge so we manage risks around people loss. And how do we anticipate and consistently achieve positive outcomes for the communities we serve- customers, shareholders, the public around us. This is also where we think about the 'good corporate citizen'. In the past, of course we thought about some of these things. But we did it in isolation from each other."

Jerry turned and pointed up toward the image on the screen.

"When we start to bracket these together many of our decisions around actions look different than before. We don't see training as a cost, we see it as workforce sustainability, if we don't link that training to helping us meet the needs of our society then we miss the opportunity to sustain our market position and keep satisfied stakeholders. Hopefully this is making some sense to you?"Jerry looked around the room half expecting a question.

"Let me give you a simple real example. For months I've been hounded by a vendor to purchase a training programme on using a particular software product to improve efficiency. The product is an application for creating and publishing documents. It's a common thing found on many people's computers. I have never seen any demand or need for it I so I've been pushing back. We could be spending the money on other things.

"A thought was raised by one of Susan's team as we discussed what sort of things we could do to make a positive impact at the same time in all three of the elements in this Triple Knot."

He nodded in acknowledgement toward Leila who was sitting with the other team members.

"Did you know that we used a lot of whiteout in some areas where redaction is required for privacy purposes etc? We print a copy of a document, whiteout the area we need to, scan it back in and save it as a new redacted document. Well, now we don't. Instead, we bring up the original, make an electronic copy, use the edit tools in this application to redact text and resave it as an updated and redacted version. Simple? No printing, no scanning, no whiteout.

"A simple thing like this has made the work cheaper, environmentally more positive as we are printing a hell of a lot less, and a lot easier for staff who were frustrated by what we did before. In other words. A positive for all three elements at the same time."

Jerry shook his head. "Seems really dumb that we hadn't changed to this practice before but quite honestly, until we started to think about all three areas we just did what we'd always done. How many more opportunities to improve are there for us to take?

"Now I'm not suggesting this is the breakthrough. What I am saying though, is that now, having looked at our business in this way, we check all of our proposed plans to see if they will positively impact the three domains and most likely give those ones that do, priority over other proposals." Jerry could see that the Board were listening carefully to what he was saying.

Sue. One of the Board. held up a hand. "Can I ask then what the major initiatives are that you will be implementing from this work? It sounds as though the team have done a lot of work in revoking at priorities."

"The upshot of the work we are doing is that we are now in the process of developing up a new scorecard that ties these elements together into an Organisational Sustainability report with metrics that we are sure puts us in front of the game and enables us to take early action if things aren't going too well.

"There are two other major initiatives coming out of our discussion around this Triple Knot. The first is to establish a new Business Intelligence Group with expertise in setting up our data needs, gathering strategies and reporting. We believe that we can set this up from within our current reporting and analysis functions within our separate business units. For example, I have an HR analyst and I would move that resource into this team. It does mean a new role of Manager for the team and we are currently drafting that role description up now.

"The second initiative is very much linked but it is to start the process of educating our teams in the importance of thinking outside of the perspective of our expert disciplines. Building the whole organisation to be more conscious of the Sustainability Triple Knot. We've already started asking managers to show how different business unit projects will contribute to the three areas."

Jerry paused and looked over toward the Board members. He noticed a couple of frowns.

" I see some of you look like you may have questions?" he asked.

Brian, a board member who had been with the organisation for several years cleared his throat.

"Hmm. I am intrigued at the notion of the Business Intelligence Group. Can you you tell us a bit more about how you think it will help? I mean, if you are doing stuff now, then why not just get your current folk pointed slightly differently ? In a manner of speaking."

"Thanks Brian. " said Jerry. "I'm glad you asked this. We had quite a discussion regarding the idea. It was actually Susan who suggested this and to be honest we were all quite skeptical in the beginning. I have to say now that I wish it was my idea. As mentioned, we will be looking to 'redirect' the focus of people we already have but we will need greater muscle to make it work. Hence the addition of a manager, and some new analysis and reporting tools. Perhaps Susan would like to add to this?"

Susan smiled as she left her seat and headed to the podium.

"Thanks Jerry. Actually though. It wasn't my idea. In the last organisation I worked at our CEO drove this. He had a Masters degree in Strategic Information Systems and he was always banging on about how 'unstrategic' information inside companies actually is.

"He set up a group to define new 'lead' metrics rather than what he called 'lags'. He said that even though there was some use in having some reports as they were, he didn't think they helped the business determine any real courses of action until it was too late. For example, the monthly staff turnover that was discussed by the exec team at the monthly meetings. His view was that once a person had decided to leave, it was too late to do anything. Of course there is a large cost to turnover and he believed that it was critical to try and understand what the future of retention might look like in a few months. He wanted something that could help his team try to address possible reasons for key people leaving before it was too late.

"He had two sayings he used all the time, "Don't tell me what's happened. Tell me what's going to happen." and his other favourite. "We can't control what's already passed but we may be able to influence the future."

Another board member, Michael, leaned forward in his seat. "Did it work? Did he get the information he needed? It seems like a big ask."

Susan nodded slowly. "Actually. He did get quite a bit of change in this space. It was during my last 6 months there but I definitely felt that we had more forward focused conversations about things than we we were having before we shifted our thinking. It wasn't easy though."

"Thanks Susan. Just out of interest though, what did you start measuring to get in front of the retention issue?"

Susan smiled and looked around. "Well. It was perhaps a little inelegant technically, but actually it seemed to really help our conversations around building meaningful ways to stop losing staff. The HR analyst in the Business Intelligence Group produced a questionnaire guide (with a form) for managers. Every manager would complete this form after their monthly one on one sessions with their staff members. During those coaching conversations each manager needed to enquire, sensitively of course, about how the employee was feeling about what we know are main drivers for exiting. Things such as, lack of training, opportunities for growth etc. Managers then had to provide their report to the HR analyst who compiled it and looked for trends etc. As I say. Not the most elegant thing, but it worked. It also forced managers to actually have meaningful conversations with their team members," she laughed

"The lack of which, is one of the main reasons, apparently, that people leave their jobs," quipped Michael.

There was silence for a moment and then Jerry spoke up.

"I have been involved to a large degree in the other lines of work that we are presenting today, as ultimately, they all have relationships to our people strategies. I ask you all to look for some of those connections as we go forward. I know Moris will spend a bit more time on this but it is a point that we can't lose sight of."

Jerry could see Mara pointing toward her wrist to indicate time.

"I'm also very conscious of time and I don't want to be the one who puts us behind schedule so if there are no other questions?" he looked around... "Then perhaps we can move onto the next presentation."

CHAPTER 17

A NEW WORKPLACE DESIGN

T he room was silent.

Leo moved toward the podium and then hesitated. He looked around the room and motioned to both Gordon and Shona to join him. Which they did. Gordon perhaps a little more reluctantly than Shona, who strode forward as though she were a key note speaker.

"Hello everyone. I've asked Gordon and Shona to join me here as I think it important that we all understand that exploring this particular Triple Knot has given us a fantastic example of the power of different views working together on something that none of us alone could do. I'll apologise to both of my compadres here as they didn't know I was going to do this but I do think it is really important that you understand how doing this in the way we have has already changed a lot of my views. I want to acknowledge the contribution of these two in particular for that. Besides. I know I don't have all of the answers to the questions that may come our way and I'm hoping they can help answer some of those." Leo grinned.

"I'm sure you all know Gordon. Our head of Operations?" he waited and saw nods all round. "Well this is Shona, our Organisational Development consultant, who works within Jerry's team. Shona has a deep knowledge of ways to get disparate teams working well together.

She has also helped us hugely in gathering and analysing human data to help us formulate our plans."

Shona smiled at the audience and saw appreciative nods and smiles from many of them.

"Now. I'll try and be like Jerry and be as brief and concise as possible. Again though, please feel free to ask or comment to myself or my colleagues here.

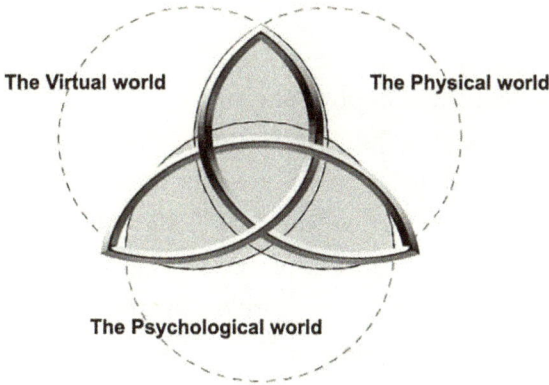

The Virtual world

The Physical world

The Psychological world

"We have been looking at the Workplace Triple Knot. Leo indicated the slide that came up on the screen behind him.

"This describe's today's world of work. And life. Basically, work is no longer just a physical place you go to do things. It is actually three separate, yet very interrelated domains. You can see from the Triple Knot diagram that there is a Physical Workspace - which nowadays could be anywhere, from home, office, hotel room…There is also a Digital, or Virtual Workspace which is the world of social media, internet, devices etc. Then there is the Psychological Workplace that each of us carry privately within us.

"I'm being as simplistic as I can here but all three of these worlds, and we use that term purposely, have changed and are changing at a very rapid rate. Each of them can have major impacts on the other."

Leo looked at Gordon who nodded, and indicated that he should continue.

"You'll note from the diagram that there are dotted lines around each of these which is indicating that they extend out further than just the Workplaces. This is to show that each of these worlds are actually also the worlds we live in, not just work in, and the lines between work and life are getting more blurred everyday. For example, hybrid working means a lot more work is done in the home perhaps and outside of standard 'office' times. It means more flexibility is needed in the employment relationship. I'll pause there for any thoughts or questions."

Gail Downs, one of the newer board members held up her hand. Leo indicated that she should go ahead.

" This is fascinating," she remarked. "I think it clearly shows the complexities needed to be considered nowadays in designing the workplace. Are you saying that when you design the office for example, you need to consider the impact on the other two 'worlds' and spend time perhaps doing some design work on them?"

Leo nudged Shona to respond.

"Well. Yes. That's exactly what we are saying. Not only that though. We have to think beyond the work into the life of our employees. If we don't then we could end up putting things in place that have a negative impact on their... mental wellbeing or perhaps personal security whilst working digitally."

Gail looked around at her fellow board members. " This seems to me to be extremely important for us especially as Directors. We have a duty of care that I'm not entirely sure we can be totally confident of living up to when you consider the implications of this."

Maureen looked very thoughtful as she added, " Yes. Looking at things this way puts a whole new perspective on Health, Safety and Wellness. Can you tell us more about where this Triple Knot is taking you?"

"Gordon?" prompted Leo.

"Ah....yes. Um, we decided that trying to encompass everything at once was potentially too big for our poor little heads to get around. So we have adopted a simple two stage plan to take us forward."

Leo put up a new slide that had a few bullet points:

Stage One

* Try and define clearly, what a desired future state might look like

* Identify the gap between that future state and what we currently have in place.

Stage Two

* Develop action plans to change from current state to future state.

* Implement and monitor

Gordon continued. "I know this looks very….basic. But we just needed something to help us stay focused and these four steps have become our compass. They have helped us to maintain our drive when we have been in danger of stalling, or going down deep rabbit holes. Almost a mantra, at times.

"One thing though that is really important here, is how we have approached this. We have adopted a high involvement approach. We've invited any staff interested, to become involved. This doesn't mean meetings of large numbers. We have a core team who have been responsible for pulling things together into understandable and digestible chunks but we have set up information sessions where other staff can contribute, question, or just learn what is happening. I've actually been a bit blown away by how many staff come to these sessions and are interested."

Gail raised her hand again.

"Yes Gail?" Gordon indicated she should go ahead.

"What sort of things did staff come up with?"

Gordon looked over at Leo who inclined his head suggesting "keep going."

"Well. I'm really glad you asked that. I think the best example is from right at the start. We were actually stuck on the first point in trying to understand what a desired future state might look like.

"One of our procurement team mentioned that they had worked in Amsterdam a few years ago in a workplace that was quite different. They said they loved it and would have stayed except they had to move as their partner got promoted back here. Their view was that the company had created a physical workplace that was designed around the employee's needs and catered for all three of these workspaces, physical, virtual and psychological.

"We simply thought, why try to reinvent what works and so Shona took up the challenge and tracked all of this down. I have to say we were pretty excited by what she found and so we believe now that it is part of the strategy for us to implement. It's good that we are talking to you now because it does mean quite a different way of working and the board will need to understand it if, as we would like, you are to support it."

Gail smiled. "This just gets more intriguing by the minute. So what did you find Shona?"

Shona cleared her throat and answered. "Firstly. This isn't the silver bullet. But I think it's pretty damn close and would gain us a heck of a lot if we can implement it well." She looked down and took a deep breath. "It's a thing called Activity Based Working. ABW. Rather a boring name but basically it's about creating workspaces around the different types of main activities that people undertake. It's more of a human needs approach to designing the workplace than a space driven approach, if you like.

"It's been around for a few years now but for some reason it hasn't been well communicated and many people have only heard of some aspects that, by themselves, can seem to be a bit of a turnoff. Hard to explain but I will say that the organisations I visited who have implemented this well rave about it. Staff and managers. What I have learned about this has really opened my eyes as to what a contemporary organisation should look like."

"So if ABW is so good. Why hasn't this thing really taken off do you think?" asked Michael

"Great question. In fact. I asked exactly the same thing. Tony Delahunt thinks there are a number of reasons but he believes the main thing is that it was originally promoted as just an office design. Mis-promoted is what he actually said. It was way before Covid and the focus really was on designing a physical office space where people could work more effectively and efficiently. That means the focus was given more around the physical environment and perhaps slightly less so on the technological and psychological environments. I have to say now that I have studied it more I have to agree with him."

The entire board were leaning forward in their seats as Gail jumped in again.

"So how would it be different for us? Why would we do this?"

Shona frowned and chewed on her bottom lip for a moment. She looked over to Leo who nodded and smiled supportively, and then across to Jerry, sitting with the audience. He raised both thumbs.

"Actually. I think we have a real opportunity here to seriously propel the business forward. Not too long ago I was a lot more skeptical but if we really want to build a contemporary and sustainable business then I think this path offers us the very best chance of success. The world of work has changed a lot over the last decade as things like flexible work, hybrid work and life-work balance are key drivers. ABW, if we widen our view to include, for instance, the home offices of hybrid workers, would mean that we would build a much stronger and enduring relationship with our people. More than that. It will increase productivity, lower costs and give us a lot more flexibility to adapt faster as the operating environment changes."

"Wow. That sounds like an advert." quipped Michael.

"Perhaps," responded Shona. "But I will say that this is the first time in a long time that I've actually been excited about the prospect of a newly designed and appropriate way of working. Up till now, I feel as though we've been locked into a model that was designed by military and churches." She looked over to Jerry and Moris and smiled. "And seriously. We can't expect things to be different if we just keep doing the same things again and again. We NEED to do something radical." Shona was so forceful with this last point that several members of the board looked at each other in surprise.

"Ah. I'll jump in here now," suggested Leo.

"I see a little bit of surprise. What Shona is referring to is how in the past, organisation design has followed structures and processes and operating models based around a different mindset. More... hierarchical, perhaps. Now I know we could spend a lot more time on this one aspect but I'd like to suggest we move onto what we recommend we actually do. I'm sure that if anyone wants to know more about ABW then we can have a chat offline later. Is that OK?"

It looked like both Gail and Michael had questions and they both looked at each other and laughed. They sat back in their chairs shaking their heads.

"So I guess you can see that one of our recommendations is to start going down this ABW line. By the way, we think we should call it something different but that is detail to consider later.

"Just so you understand though. Doing this will mean likely redesign of not only our physical workplace but also many of our practices and policies. It will definitely mean a shift in culture for the company and that is something that is actually a whole Triple Knot subject for discussion later today as well.

"We also want to explore more deeply, the area of psychological safety in particular and what that means for our workforce. It's something a bit dark and mysterious and certainly is different than what I grew up in. Especially in terms of the company's responsibilities and responses.

"Suffice to say, that it feels like a bit of a quagmire at times trying to understand this whole area."

There were a lot of nods.

"Last but not least, our third major recommendation leans heavily into the area that Jerry and Susan discussed. That is, the creation of a Business Intelligence Group to help us establish and monitor real information relevant to how we are performing in making this Triple Knot effective."

Moris stood up and moved over toward the podium.

"I'm really sorry everyone but time is critical today and I know you have many questions. Can I ask though that we try to get through the presentations and then over the next few weeks we can refine our documents with feedback etc?"

Gail nodded. "Yes. I'm ok with that and I have to say this looks like something I'll be very keen to learn more about. Thank you Leo and team." she gave a nod back at Moris.

"I think it is time for a short break. There is tea and coffee and some nice sugary biscuits to keep our energy up although given what I've seen so far, I don' think energy will be an issue. Can we perhaps take say 15 minutes and then come back in for the rest of the sessions?"

As people got up to leave Moris added, "Feel free to bring your refreshments back into the auditorium with you. I'm sorry for the tight timeframes but we do have a lot of material to get through. Thanks," he indicated the exits out to the foyer.

As he exited Moris noticed Wiremu standing next to the wall opposite, chatting with Jerry who waved Moris over.

"I have news," Wiremu announced as Moris came closer.

"They have decided not to pursue any personal grievance and have asked that both parties just let everything drop."

Moris frowned and shook his head in disbelief. "That's it? They expect that we will accept that?"

Wiremu glanced at Jerry and gave a half nod. "Pretty much. Yes. I do have a view and so does Jerry. I think the two of us probably are in synch."

"And?" queried Moris looking at both of them.

"Well. I think No. We shouldn't accept that. At the end of the day a staff member looks to have defrauded the business and tried to cover their tracks by framing you for it. They've also initiated a smear campaign on social media. Again, I think, to cover their activities. My advice is that we hand this over to the Police and let them go for it," said Wiremu.

Jerry nodded. "The forensic accountant working with Susan's team will have all of the documentation ready for the Police soon."

Moris looked at his watch and sighed. "OK. Even though we really don't need more drama right now, I think we have to go ahead. I'm about to talk later today about shifting to a deeper level of leadership and that means being prepared to take some tough action when it is warranted. I think it is in this case. Can I leave the details up to you two? I need a few minutes to brief Maureen before we go back in."

Wiremu said, "Just leave it with me for now. I know Jerry is keen to be in that room with you today. I can handle it for you."

Moris sighed, "Thanks. Let's catch up tomorrow." He signalled to Maureen that he needed a couple of minutes and joined her as she re-entered the auditorium. The two of them went into a corner and spoke quietly together for a few minutes as everyone else came in and took their seats.

CHAPTER 18

THE EMPLOYMENT VALUE PROPOSITION

"Thank you all for being so, on time." There were a few chuckles. In a few minutes, everyone was seated and Moris looked around the room. He could almost feel the positive expectations. He smiled.

"So far today we have heard from a couple of teams who have been working with Triple Knot thinking. We do have a bit more of this but before we go into that I just want to impress again, the idea of connections between each Triple Knot as that is something we need to have clear. The overall outcome of this work, is likely to be a significant new operating model. That is where this is taking us and I am sure that you will see the simple logic behind it all. We should go into this with our eyes open, understanding as much as we can, what the implications are for the business. I urge you to continue to be engaged and ask questions or make comments.

"Now, we have a couple more Triple Knot models to show you and then I would like to wrap it up with some other thoughts that, hopefully, will resonate with you all. Thoughts that will help us to ensure any strategies we actually land on are executed in a way that facilitates success."

Moris looks over to Jerry to see if his team were ready to go. Jerry raised a thumb.

"I'd like to now hand over for a while to a small team who have been working on something that I think is very important for us today. This team has been looking at a Triple Knot view of the Employment Value Proposition. The team is different to the other teams. They have approached this mainly from the employee perspective, rather than the organisation perspective, as we have tended to do with the others.

"I'd like to introduce Brian, Qian, Amy and Mara from the HR team to lead us through this."

The team came up to the podium. All looked a little nervous. They glanced at one another and then Brian stepped forward.

"Thanks Moris," he said. "I don't mind saying that it is a little daunting standing up here and that's why we've come in numbers." There were smiles at that.

"Moris is right. We have looked at this through perhaps a different set of eyes. There is still more to be done to ensure that we are on the right track as we are also, to be fair, looking at it through our own technical HR lens. The team have been awesome in this and are very appreciative of the support that especially Moris and Jerry have given us.

"Now we aren't going to have a set of talking heads here. We just wanted you to see the faces of the team and understand who we are. I've drawn the short straw and will do the presenting but I do invite any of the team to jump in whenever."

Brian turned toward the screen behind him and waited for the slide to come up.

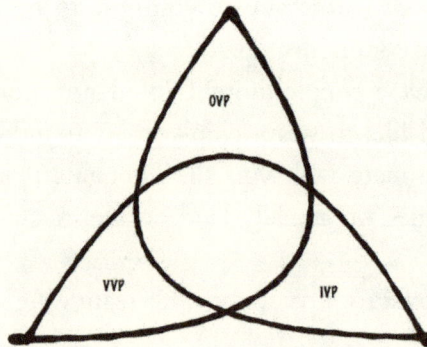

THE EMPLOYMENT VALUE PROPOSITION

"Some of you may have heard the term, 'Employee Value Proposition."

There were one or two nods around the room.

"Well to be honest. I've always felt that conversations about this thing were quite shallow. When this team started to discuss it, we found that we all felt the same way. It seems to have been driven out of recruitment environments and has always focused on what the employee can get out of an employment relationship with an employer. What does an employer have to offer in terms of conditions of employment, or nice environment etc.

"In effect. What can you offer that the folks down the road can't?

"We think that is a bit one dimensional. And to be fair, we are generalising a bit. Our view, is that idea of an Employee Value Proposition has been very limiting and misses the target.

"You'll also notice that we have called this 'EmployMENT Value Proposition. Changing the emphasis from Employee to *Employment*. That's because we think that this thing is bigger and wider than the recruitment offering."

Brian pointed up towards the screen. " This Triple Knot suggests that there is not one but three, inter-related employment propositions that together establish whether an employment relationship between an employer and employee will work.

"Firstly we have VVP. Vocational Value Proposition. This is about the kind of work you want to do. For example, a teacher or a police officer or a dentist or,... whatever. Even an HR Advisor! Something attracts you to a particular type of work.

"There is something about the actual work that resonates with you. For some people that really limits where they can work. But it's the old saying 'If you do what you really love, you'll never work a day in your life' Or something like that."

There was murmurs of agreement around the room.

"Well. Do we really have any idea why or what it is that our people really love to do? Not really, but we do think we need to really get onto this if we are to be able to help fulfil that for people.

"The second proposition area is OVP. Organisational Value Proposition. Which organisation do I want to join, where I get to do what I love to do? Many of us have choices. As an HR person I can work in almost any organisation. But do I want to work for say,... an arms manufacturer? The public sector? The private sector?

"The big question for us. Do we know why *our* organisation attracts people? Is it what we do? How we do it? Or what we stand for? Are we socially responsible? Are we helping others?

"I know there are a lot of questions here but that's the point. We don't currently have answers to them. We should, if we are to be really competitive and want to keep great employees."

Brian paused for just a moment and then continued. "The third part of this model is the Individual Value Proposition. IVP. This describes what the Individual gets out of the relationship in terms of benefits to them. Now the thing with this is that organisations haven't been great at understanding that individual staff have different needs, wants and desires. Traditionally, we've looked at putting a one size fits all kind of terms and conditions package together. It's less complicated and ultimately probably cheaper to administer. But it doesn't hit the mark"

Michael spoke up. "But surely this is the area we know most about. And can actually control. Right? There's tons of research out there that tells us what is important to different generations. Money for mortgage, kid friendly policies and growth opportunities for younger generations and perhaps interesting work and healthcare benefits etc for the older, more experienced workers? I know I am generalising but for example, the money would likely be less of an issue to the older workers without mortgages than it is to a young family staring out. Yes?"

Brian looked over to Qian who had put her hand up to respond. "Please. Go ahead Qian" he said.

Qian spoke up. "I thought that too. Especially as everywhere you look people promote the generational stuff and we get told it every day. Well, guess what? I was discussing this exact thing with Tony at lunch when he was at one of our meetings. He suggested I look at some research done by some NZ academics. Actually. That research and others I have seen since don't support the popular myths about GenX, Boomers, Millenials etc. None. In fact, the opposite is true. There is a lot of research showing that there are very few differences in these workforces."

"Seriously? " questioned Michael. "I thought that with all of the information around about the generations, that we had a really good handle on things. You're saying it isn't true?"

"I know! Right!" said an excited Qian. "We were surprised as well. When you actually dig into things you'll notice that actually, attitudes and values are still the same as they've always been. It's the conditions and the context that changes. Not the people. Stereotyping generations is just pop culture."

Michael looked at Maureen and raised his eyebrows. He returned his focus to Qian and asked, "So, what have you discovered?"

"What has been different is the environments in which we all live and work in. The context. There are a lot of variables, and labelling generations isn't helping. Consider for example how many parents re-mortgage, reasonably late I life, to assist their kids buy homes. Money is still important."Also, how many couples both work in a household today compared to 30 years ago?"

"It's not that simple. We believe that we really should be trying somehow, to personalise our offerings, based on what we have discovered about our individual people, as much as we can. Imagine an employer who can do that. I'll use myself as an example. I would be labelled as a Gen Z. Works for money, generally lazy, entitled. No loyalty to an employer. It's not true.

"I am actually quite well off financially as my parents set up accounts for me from a very young age. Jerry knows this. He knew that giving me a bonus like others get at the end of a year is kind of…well ho hum."

"I'll take it. " mumbled Brian.

Qian glared at him and he raised his hands.

"Do you know that last year, instead of a bonus, he arranged for me and my dog to spend a few days at a puppy retreat where we both learned how to live together well? It cost about the same as the bonus I would have got and I suppose I could have done that myself. The point is though that I was blown away by the fact that he did that. He showed that he knew me and understood that I would value that."

Michael pursed his lips, nodded, and then sat back in his chair with a thoughtful look. "Wow." he silently mouthed and looked over toward Jerry with a smile.

"Thanks Qian." said Brian. "How difficult would it be to have an element of our reward system based around the individual? This is a tricky area. But we really think that we need to put more effort into knowing our people and if possible, building a modern reward system that fits them better. Just doing what the guys down the road are doing isn't making a difference. Our first major recommendation is exactly that. We need to build a better system of knowing our people, and secondly we need to try and design enough around the differences to meet their aspirations and needs. That's going to take some careful thought.

"Our second recommendation is to initiate more robust workforce planning to identify the kinds of roles we will need for the future so that we can begin to understand more about the Vocational Value Proposition and tapping into that to attract the best candidates.

"The OVP will be created as a result of all of the work we have talked about today and probably most especially the work going on with the next Triple Knot. Can I ask? Are there any questions or comments?"

Brian looked at the team as well as around the room.

Maureen started to clap and very soon the room was filled with light applause from nearly everyone.

Moris stepped back up to the podium and thanked the team.

"Well. I think you can see that things are really diving deep and some great thinking is going on," he said.

CHAPTER 19

A COMPLEX KNOT

"The last Triple Knot is one that I have struggled a little more with. Not because it's difficult to comprehend. But rather, you have to get your head around the ramifications of this particular one. This Knot underpins success in all of our other Triple Knots. Jerry's team have been doing the leg work on this to help us stay on track but essentially, this Triple Knot is one that the leadership team needs to really own and drive. It also needs to be something for the Board to get more comfortable with, and support."

Moris frowned thoughtfully as he spoke.

"What I'm talking about is the Triple Knot of a High Performance Culture. Ultimately, and I think we all understand this. Unless we get this bit right, everything else will fail. That's why the leadership needs to completely own it.

"Now I'm not going to go into the theoretical model. Tony has already covered that with both the Board and in much more detail with the SLT.

"What I am going to do is firstly remind you of what the Knot looks like, and then I want to spend some time talking about what we, the senior people, need to do, or think about, in order to make it all work."

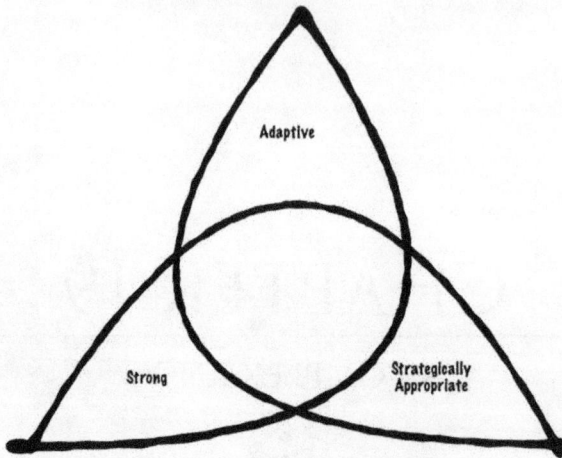

A slide appeared on the screen behind Moris.

"The High Performance Culture is one that embodies these three core dimensions." Moris turned and indicated toward the screen.

"The Culture needs to be Adaptive, in order to constantly anticipate and adjust, to shifts in the world around it. History is littered with great companies who have not been able to change when needed and have become victims of their own intractability.

"Secondly, the Culture needs to be Strong throughout the organisation so that there is a shared and consistent sense of purpose and what is really important, in terms of how we do things.

"The third part of this is the Strategically Appropriateness of the culture to the world in which we operate. By that I mean, the type of business we are, the kind of people we engage as employees, and the expectations of the stakeholders we need to look after."

In his sharp blue suit, crisp white open necked shirt and confident stance, Moris was holding the audience attention very well indeed. He really looked like a CEO on a mission.

"Our assessment of the company against this model suggests that we aren't doing particularly well in any of the three factors.

"The work that Jerry and his team, have been doing, guided by Tony, has really helped us to understand how we measure and understand what our culture could, and should, look like.

"We have a fairly clear picture of the gap between how we would describe our culture now. for each of these dimensions, and how we would like it to be. Our plan essentially, then, is to execute initiatives that will enable us to bridge that gap. We've been putting our heads together identifying and designing those initiatives."

You could just about hear a pin drop. Everyone was listening so closely.

"Before I launch into what we are thinking, I just want to stress again how critical the work on getting the 'right' culture for us is. I'm going to be asking you, the Board, to support us even though some of you might not be comfortable with aspects of our approach."

He looked at the board members and waited for a moment before carrying on. He could feel a heightened level of nervousness and anticipation in the room as he took a deep breath ready to carry on.

"All of you, at some stage, have likely been involved in some sort of culture change programme"

He looked around and saw lots of nodding.

"These programmes, generally, have followed a similar formula. We believe that formula has lost it's relevance nowadays."

Gail raised her hand. She looked confused. "What do you mean? Lost it's relevance. You've just told us that we need to undergo culture change."

"We do," said Moris.

"Let me explain. Anyone of the SLT please feel free to chip in. Generally, culture change programmes follow a similar pattern. They aim to create and build on a set of company Values that staff can engage with and we can use to refer to in how we behave as an organisation. Usually, you end up with a statement or something that describes who you are (as a company) and what is important to you. Tony would say mostly it is a set of phrases or words to describe the Strategically Appropriate part of the Triple Knot.

"Programmes are built to get staff buy in and engagement to these values and HR try and build the values into policies and practices around reward, recruitment performance etc. To make the Strong part of the Triple Knot work.

"We think the days of Value statements is over. People just don't want them anymore. They worked in the 90s and 2000s and that was fine but now the world has changed. People are actually quite cynical of statements. Plus, I know that there are enough of the 'old guard' staff here who would likely think, here we go again, and pass their mistrust and cynicism onto the newer staff."

Some of the Board turned to look at each other.

"I have seen many values statements over the years. I've helped shaped them. I have always, though, felt a little uncomfortable with them and I think I now understand why. Sometimes I feel they are bit condescending and I can feel mildly insulted when I see something like. 'Integrity' or 'Teamwork' as a company value. Why do things like that need to be spelled out? Especially to adults."

"But surely Values Statements are the easiest way to get the same message across the whole company?" challenged Gail.

"Yes that's exactly right Gail. They do get the same message across in a fairly easy way. That's part of the issue. It says to people that we see you as being all alike. It's homogenous."

Gail tilted her head back and was clearly considering this.

"The idea of Values statements originated from Military and religious organisations who became very adept at communicating what they stood for, they used symbols, slogans, Values statements etc. And they did it well. They still do. Shona talked about this earlier."

He looked over to the HR team and saw Shona sit up straighter in her seat.

"Now I would like you to just think about the results of the clear messaging. People who were aligned with the espoused values and beliefs joined. Those organisations have been very adept at getting alignment amongst their people. In fact, if you really look. You'll notice that many of the people in this organisations look the same, talk the same, and act the same."

A slide appeared behind him showing a room full of middle aged men in military uniforms sitting in an auditorium They all clearly looked alike.

Gail chuckled at this.

Moris stepped away from the podium as he continued. It was going well. He knew this and he also knew it was time to push it further.

"The ultimate in alignment. Well, we don't want to attract the same model. I'm not saying values etc are wrong. But I am saying that we need to modernise and contemporise our approach so that we can reach and engage a much more diverse group of people who can feel included for their differences, not necessarily their similarities.

"Are we all ok with what I've just said?" He looked around hoping for someone to talk. Eventually, Maureen spoke up as she looked at her fellow board members. "I think so. Yes."

"These type of organisations are steeped in hierarchy. That's ok. In the past, so were a lot of organisations in the business world. The Corporate Values statement is a legacy of that world."

He saw quite a few nods. Including some of the board.

"The sustainable High Performance Culture we need can't be that hierarchical model. That just won't cut it for today's world. The really hard question though. Is, what will cut it?"

Moris could feel himself flowing through this presentation. His words were clear and unhurried and he could tell were hitting the mark.

"The SLT had many deep discussions about this and I have to say that we were often more in violent agreement than disagreement. We know that we need to be more deliberate about building and shifting to a High Performance Culture. We also strongly believe that we have do it in a different way to what has been done in the past, in order for us to be successful.

"One thing SLT all agreed to was that we didn't want some slick, slogan riddled, over engineered culture change project to eat our brains. As Leo politely put it - no amount of fluffy, cuddly psycho-mumbo jumbo will shift hearts and minds of network engineers and developers."

There was a snort of amusement from the area where the Board were sitting.

"Our major design principle is to keep things, simple, clear and real.

"We asked ourselves the question of what we thought our ideal culture should look like. How could we describe it in a way that is easy to understand? We did this because that's our role. We should be providing direction and guidance. At a workshop facilitated by Tony Delahunt we tried to be as clear and straightforward as possible. I gotta say this isn't easy when you have roomful of management people!"

"And HR Folk!" trumpeted Leo from a seat in the back.

That elicited a couple of giggles. Mainly from the HR folk.

Moris carried on.

"Eventually we came up with a list of the things we said we wanted the company to be. Now this list is ours. We can choose how to use it. Hanging it on the wall in a fancy frame doesn't get others into it. Instead, we believe that we need to start doing some things differently and each of us signalling within our own areas what we believe and why. Management-speak across the company doesn't cut it. Small groups. Tribes, if you like. Can get a heck of a lot more by having open conversations, in their own special language." Moris really stressed that last bit.

"Doing this will invite people into using their own frames of reference to get a greater understanding of what we think and why. I can see Jerry for example, using different narratives, than Leo to get some level of understanding from their teams. Assuming that IT folk get turned on by the same words as HR folk is a bridge too far." He grinned.

Maureen raised her hand."I have a question," she said

"Sure. Go ahead Maureen," said Moris

"This still sounds like you have drafted a set of values. I can't quite picture what's different. Can you elaborate perhaps?"

"Okay. But I don't want us to get lost in words and definitions and detail. What we ended up with is something that we thought captured our conversation as a group as to what we thought the company culture would look like if we were doing well in each of the Triple Knot areas.

"The need to be Adaptive is clear. But being Resilient for instance was something we thought described an organisation that could handle adversity, that staff were able and psychologically prepared to deal with difficulties. We think that is Strategically Appropriate for our business today. It's not the only thing that we came up with but the point is, what we came up with was what the *SLT* believes will bring the company success. It's also the things that SLT can have an impact on."

Maureen looked very thoughtful.

"Now we haven't described these words in any depth or attributed any explanations as to what we mean by them. These aren't for everyone else. Although we are happy to share. Our strategy, rather than putting out a corporate poster, is to engage in team based discussions on what success looks like. What we need to achieve as a business. We want to invite employees to help us build the plans to make achievement real. We want our teams to build their own understandings and definitions of values that have meaning for *them* in *their* work and will contribute to what success means for them. Engineering, for example, could well come up with a different set of words than Customer Services.

"The real power of this process is the conversation itself. Not the words that we produce. Teams need dedicated time and space to discuss and understand each others views and ideas until they land on the things that they feel collectively, are the most important in contributing to overall organisation success. You can't get that level of engagement from a set of words somebody else gives you."

Moris slowly looked about the room before adding.

"We really want to make this work and that means shifting gears in a way that recognises the diversity of staff and the need to involve them in important conversations."

He paused again and carefully watched the reactions of the Board especially.

Moris could see that everyone was really taking this in and thinking hard about what he was saying.

He glanced up toward the SLT and noticed that they too, were watching the Board. He decided to continue on.

"Ultimately though. It isn't what we say is important. It's what we do. The leadership, and management, need to accept that we are actually the climate control regarding culture. To that end, it is critical that we act in ways that positively affect the outcomes we are after. If we think that Resilience is important, then it is up to us to build it.

"We therefore are undertaking an ambitious programme of leadership development for all of the SLT and some high potential managers to ensure that we are working in a way that sets and maintains that climate control for culture. It is our actions and our behaviours that will make the difference. Not exhortations of our staff to do better."

Sue, from the Board raised a hand and Moris signalled for her to proceed.

"This is fascinating. I must say I think the team has really thought about things very well indeed. I am interested though in the leadership development programme you have chosen. I'm not aware myself of any that focus on this angle."

Moris smiled and shook his head. "Actually Sue. This is new. It's something which at this stage will actually be bespoke. The reason for that is that it concentrates on building our capability around a concept known as Deep Leadership. It focuses on helping us to develop our ability to 'Cultivate' others. It builds on the work of Daniel Goleman and has been conceived and designed by Tony Delahunt. I won't go into detail today but I am happy to discuss it with any Board members at any time."

He paused. Cocked his head to one side and asked. "Shall I move us on? I'm sorry but we are in danger of running over time today and this was really designed to give you a feel for the direction we are taking rather than the detail of everything. I think it may be time for me to summarise and close off for the day."

"Please." said Michael. "Otherwise we are in danger of eating fluffy mumbo-jumbo. Or something like that."
Everyone laughed.

Moris indicated for the next slide. "To summarise then," he said

"Today. We have looked at four different Triple Knots and talked about adopting a fairly radical approach to building a more fit for purpose operating model.

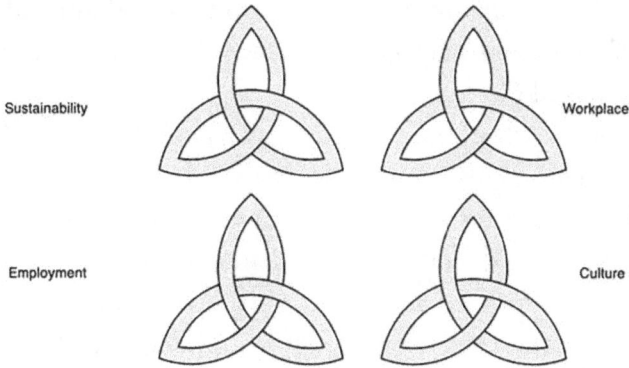

Sustainability

Workplace

Employment

Culture

"I don't want to overly complicate things but I have been grappling with this idea for a while. I think the work we did on the individual Triple Knot areas is all good, but the real key in terms of building it as an organisational system is when we connect them together. They are actually connected anyway. But my view is that we need to try and connect them more by design than by accident. The circle in the middle is us. A Collective Leadership team. Making sure the connections are working well.

"Together, these knots make up the core of what we need to consider in order to have a great overall and enduring operating model. They don't describe the systems and policies and processes etc that we have to have as major enablers. That's on us. The SLT. We are the group who ensure that interconnectedness is working."

Sustainable

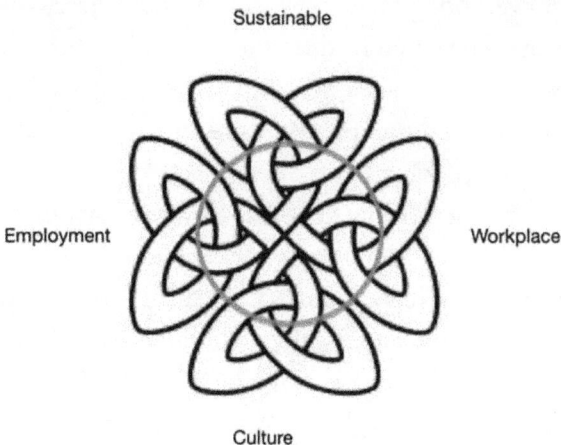

Employment

Workplace

Culture

Moris let this sink in. He stood behind the podium and held the silence. He felt that to say anything now would just compromise the impact he hoped this had.

Gail and Michael both raised their hands. Maureen glanced at them and then watched Moris as he squared his shoulders.

Michael spoke first. "I get it. Shit Moris," he leaned forward. "I really like it," he said, and then looked around to see if others agreed.

Gail leaned forward also and cupped her chin with both hands. "This is different. I have to say though. And I don't often do….I agree with Michael. This is somehow both complex and simple. It's hard to describe but I really, really like what you and the team have come up with."

At that, Moris smiled, as people started to applaud.

≈

It was a small, cosy restaurant and bar. Moris, Jerry and Maureen were having a quiet drink. They'd had dinner with the board and the rest of the leadership team. Leo had to leave early as he had a squash tournament on and needed to be at the court at least half and hour before his first game. He said he felt invigorated by today and reckoned he was up for a big win.

Susan and Gordon had each made lame excuses about needing to rest before a big day tomorrow. They left together. Completely unaware that everybody knew they were an item. Jerry quipped, after they'd gone, of course, that he didn't really think either of them would get much rest.

"Quite a day," commented Maureen.

"Indeed," agreed Moris.

"What's next then? How does this all move forward?" questioned Maureen

Moris glanced at Jerry and said "Well. To be honest, we don't think this is going to be an easy ride. We're realists. There is still a lot of groundwork to do before we really start building."

He looked down at his glass. " We have some real work to do still on changing our own approach to leading. I talked with you awhile ago about the notion of the Cultivator leader. I'm determined that we get this and begin to set the way we handle the building of resilience and management of expectations more realistically."

"I know what you mean. Ever since we spoke I've become much more aware of the dangers of what has been promoted as best diversity and inclusion practice. I've really started to look at our younger workers and worry that we've been building the opposite of what we should be."

Jerry grinned at this and said, "This is music to my heart."

They sat in silence for while, each lost in their own thoughts.

Maureen put her glass down and said. "I really better be going soon but I honestly do want to congratulate you all. I think the logic and rational approach today has really given the Board confidence that we are on the right track.

"Also, quite pleased with the outcome of the Averil situation. I just don't get why anyone would do the things she did." Maureen shook her head. "So what's the plan to fill the role? Any thoughts?"

Moris looked at Jerry. "Well, Leo reckons he's got this guy who he thinks would be absolutely perfect. His name's Derrick or Darren or something. Yes that's it. Darren."

Jerry just sat there with his head in his hands and chuckled.

EPILOGUE

"Come on Moris. Get a move on. You can't be late for this." Fiona stepped up behind him and gently took both of his shoulders in her hands to steer him away from the mirror and out the door.

"I just can't get this bloody dickie bow thing right!" protested Moris. "It won't sit straight!"

"It looks fine." Fiona said calmly. "You look great."

Moris took a deep breath and nodded. "Okay. No one's going to be looking at me anyway. You look amazing and I'm sure will outshine everybody."

Fiona giggled as she gave him a playful whack with her clutch purse. "C'mon. Let's go."

It was a beautiful clear evening that greeted them as they pulled out of the driveway and turned left toward the events centre in the middle of the city. Fiona turned on the radio in the hope that some quiet music might just help relax Moris a little.

They both laughed loudly as the sound of James Taylor singing *'How Sweet It Is To Be Loved By You'* filled the silence.

Jerry was already at the events centre but unlike Moris he was entirely comfortable in his tuxedo. Catherine was away with the kids on school camp so he had no one to tell him how he well he looked. He didn't care though. This was a big night and he was a bit nervous. Some of the HR team were enjoying themselves over at the bar and he just hoped that they stayed responsible…"Stop that!" he told himself. Let them enjoy the evening without dad frowning. He sat back in his chair and went into people watching mode. As his eyes roved around the very large and glitzy ballroom he noticed Gordon and Susan entering through the main door. He stood up and waved toward them. There were still a lot more people to come in and the place was relatively quiet as yet. Things would get going in about another 30 minutes or so.

Finally Susan spotted Jerry and waved back. She looked fantastic in a sleeveless, floor length cobalt blue gown which flared out from below knee level and hugged tight to everything above in a most attractive manner. "Lucky Gordon," thought Jerry.

Gordon didn't look so comfortable though and it was patently obvious that black tie wasn't his preferred garb for an evening out. Jerry chuckled to himself. "Why were so many men so self conscious when they scrubbed up?"

Susan and Gordon finally made their way toward Jerry after collecting some refreshments from the bar.

"Wow" said Jerry. Rising to greet them. "You look amazing," he said to Susan. Susan smiled and did a little twirl. Gordon glowered and pulled at his collar. Jerry smiled and shook his head at Gordon.

"Please. Sit. We have a while yet before things start. Fiona texted to tell me they are just parking the car downstairs. Have you seen Leo yet?" said Jerry

"He's over at the bar with that Scottish mate. Arguing about whether rugby or soccer is best. Honestly. Anyone would think they're an old married couple!"

"They are," said Jerry. "They've been married for nine years."

"What? How did I not know that!" exclaimed Gordon.

"Leo's actually fairly protective of his private life. It's not a secret. He just prefers home stuff to be home stuff."

Susan laughed and said, "Wouldn't we all."

Moris and Fiona had arrived and had joined the table. They had bumped into Maureen at the bar and brought her and her husband

Anaru over as well. It looked pretty much like the whole team were here.

Through the general hubbub of conversations around the room Maureen could just hear a little bell chiming.

"I think we'd better take our seats everyone. It sounds like we're about to get underway," she suggested.

Over the next few minutes confusion reigned as people moved around trying to find their allocated tables.

Moris and the team were all a bit jittery as the lights started to drop and people still bustled from here to there in their haste not to miss anything.

Soon though, there was relative silence as the first bars of Richard Strauss 'Also Sprach Zarathustra' started to build. Just as the fanfare reached it's climax and transitioned to the stunning Timpani the spotlight magically bathed the middle of the stage in an ethereal soft green light centred upon a man and women standing behind a very sleek and stylish lectern.

A voice boomed from the ether. "Ladies and Gentlemen. Welcome to the inaugural Prime Minister's Organisational Excellence Awards Function. Please give a warm welcome to our hosts for tonight's event. Judy and Matiu!"

There was warm applause as Judy and Matiu, a well known radio and television duo began the proceedings....

The evening was really quite enjoyable overall. The pace was kept pretty well and aside from the odd flat humour of the hosts there were a couple of very good guest speeches.

In fact. Moris thought the evening was going great. Tony's Deep Leadership programme won the award for innovation in Human Resources and as Tony wasn't there to receive the award, Jerry did so for his friend.

They were now at the point of the evening when the premier award, The Prime Minster's Award, would be announced. The team were all nervous, hopeful, but also realistic. There were some really amazing candidates in the list of finalists. Just making the final three was reward in itself after three years of hard work thought Moris.

The Prime Minister was actually here tonight and would be the person making the Award.

He stepped up to the microphone after his introduction.

"It is a real honour to be here tonight for this celebration of our country. Believe it or not, I'm not going to give any political speech tonight. Except to say that I am so very proud of how business in this country stepped up after a very difficult decade of both natural disasters and economic hardship.

"This Award was conceived out of our need as a country to regain our status. Our 'mana' and help us journey back to the great country that we have.

"Tonight we have had a number of Awards for specific disciplines and areas of work. My congratulations to all of those who won, and also to those who may not have won, but were great enough to make the competition."

There was more applause at this.

"The premier award recognises excellence across the board in all of those disciplines, as much as is possible. It is strongly based in the thinking behind the international Business Excellence Award criteria covering a range of areas that all combine to make up an entire Organisational System.

"I wish all of the finalists good luck and remind you that even if you do not take home the Prime Minister's Award you are still amazing in getting to the point of being in the top three of the country."

The Prime Minister looked around and saw Judy standing next to him with an envelope in her hand. He accepted the envelope and opened it. A smile lit his face as he read the contents of the envelope.

"Tonight we recognise a company that saw a need to be different. This organisation a few years ago, was struggling. Many were of course but this one had the courage and the foresight to step out of the known and develop it's own approach to becoming real beacon of excellence.

"In a few years, staff turnover has halved. Profitability has increased by around 30%. I'll let you read of the other key business indicators in the media tomorrow… " he joked.

The Prime Minister turned to look at the giant screen behind him.
Moris felt dizzy.
On the screen was a picture …of a giant Triple Knot.

BIBLIOGRAPHY

BOOKS

Kotter, J., Heskett, J. (1992). *Corporate Culture and Performance*. New York. The Free Press

Collins, J., Porras, J. (2000) *Built to Last* (3rd Ed). London. Random House

Collins, J. (2001) *Good to Great*. New York. HarperBusiness

Goleman, D. (2002) *Primal Leadership: Realising the Power of Emotional Intelligence*. Boston, Mass,: Harvard Business School Press

A FEW ITEMS ON SUBJECT OF GENERATIONS MYTH.

Costanza, D., Rudolph, C., Zacher, H. Nov 2023. *Are Generations a Useful Concept?* Acta Psychologica Volume 241.
https://doi.org/10.1016/j.actpsy.2023.104059

Page, B., Sept 2021. *The Generation Myth*. Research Live.
https://www.research-live.com/article/opinion/the-generation-myth/id/5089592

Minnaar, J,. Dec 2018. *Generations at work: Persistent Myths vs.*

Actual Science. Corporate Rebels. **https://www.corporate-rebels.com/blog/science-of-generations-at-work**

Murray, K., Toulson, P., Legg, S., 2011. *Generational Cohorts' expectations in the workplace: A study of New Zealanders.* AsiaPacific Journal of Human Resources.
https://doi.org/10.1177/1038411111423188